They are from Him and to Him they return.

(Qur'ān, 2, 156)

ADDRESSES II

BÜLENT RAUF

BESHARA PUBLICATIONS

© 2001, Meral Arim

ISBN 0 904975 30 4

Published by Beshara Publications
c/o Chisholme House
Roberton
Near Hawick
Roxburgh TD9 7PH

Printed in Great Britain by Antony Rowe Ltd.

Foreword

It was beside the Bosphorus, on a warm summer afternoon, people had gathered for tea. The hostess, Madame Münevver Ayaslı, turned towards an elderly Mevlevi shaykh, directing his gaze towards her cousin, and by way of introduction said: 'This is Bülent Rauf, he has thrown himself into the Ocean of the Shaykh al-Akbar and he won't come out.' The Mevlevi shaykh lowered his eyes in deference to the measure in her words and on his lips repeatedly intoned the name of God quietly to himself.

Bülent was, for many who knew him, the one who introduced them to the works of Muhyiddin Ibn 'Arabi, known as the *Shaykh al-Akbar* (the greatest teacher). Indeed, he was founder and president of the Muhyiddin Ibn 'Arabi Society, which exists to promulgate the works of this celebrated twelfth century saint.

Born into an aristocratic Ottoman family in the dying embers of the Empire, he grew up by the Bosphorus and spent the greater part of his life in cultured cosmopolitan surroundings in Europe and the Middle East. This broad canvas of experience gave him a wide and deep appreciation of life in all its varied aspects. He knew people from all shades of society, understood them and their motives, as he understood his own.

Immensely kind to everyone he met, what stood out immediately on meeting him were his impeccable manners, unaffected and not governed by habit or convention. These were the outward signs of an inner comportment from a person well used to demanding the best from himself as well as from those he loved.

A superb cook, rarely if ever did he dine alone. In fact people gathered round him not only for the light, subtle and profound conversation which swept around his table; but also for the exquisite dishes prepared and presented under his hand.

He was well aware that those who loved him found his company, though generous, sometimes awe-inspiring and difficult to bear, because he was fully present in the moment. Whereas they would be preoccupied, their attention dispersed, his was gathered, focused, and at the service of whatever the instant required. Time spent with him was always precious, acting as a mirror to shortcomings in oneself, as well as allowing one to sense that every person is a place of unlimited potential for creative expression, limited only by what they think themselves to be.

Once, when he asked how would he be remembered by those who knew him, one of those present replied that they would remember him as a simple man. He paused, then replied: 'Ah, what could there be more simple than the Divine Complexity?'

He never veered from the premise that Union with God was the sole purpose for the existence of Man, and this certainty coloured all that was accomplished through him. Those whose aim was the same, found in him one who was at ease with the most elevated explanations concerning Man's perfectibility, and who was able to express these ideas at the level of those who brought the questions. They recognised in him a source of wisdom and refinement, whose taste was always for the highest and most in accord with the essential dignity of Man. These qualities affected those who shared his company, whether students at Chisholme House in the Scottish Borders where he was Consultant to the Beshara School of esoteric education until his death in 1987, or people from a more worldly setting such as restaurateurs, academics, diplomats and aristocrats – even the market traders in his beloved Istanbul. They all found themselves in the company of a person in full possession of that essentially compassionate nature, which is in every individual as their original potential. He was the best company.

John Brass   *Oxford, May 2000*

vi

Note on the texts

While the pieces previously published in *Addresses* were mostly written for use in the Beshara School of Esoteric Education, those in the present volume arose out of more diverse circumstances during the last fifteen years of Bülent Rauf's life. Some of the shorter pieces were for use in the School, or embodied in letters written in response to particular queries, and subsequently more widely circulated. Four essays first appeared in the *Journal of the Muhyīddīn Ibn 'Arabī Society*, three in the newsletter (later the magazine) of the Beshara Trust. Thanks are due to both these bodies for permission to reprint them.

Contents

ESSENTIALS

The Essential

THE essential is not to falter from one's own essence which is The Essence. That is done by permanent, concentrated, unmitigated belief that the above premise is the only Truth, and that all that is essentially originates from that very same source. All the rest is paraphenalia, 'I feel this,' 'I feel that,' 'I have done right,' 'I have done wrong', and all such are nothing but sheer tests of the strength of your belief.

But belief must be verified, reasoned and intuited belief and conviction, not 'faith' belief or accommodation belief or belief of circumstances or because it 'seems' reasonable. It is certainly not valid, albeit sincere.

When all this is true then the tests are borne in ease, knowing well that the Essential being is ever untouched by accident or fault, nor ever is it in default. Then the tests pass over one and leave no mark or scar.

A lover has to know for certain that love is returned for love, and not for any other consideration – riches, help, comfort or bargain ...

Response to Sheer Beauty

RESPONSE to Sheer Beauty, Universal, all pervading, has to be in the same way universal, all pervading, etc. If not, then the response does not fit or suit the original uniqueness of the premise which Sheer Beauty expresses. From an individuated reality, a response in consequence of that individuation is expected. However, this depends upon the possibility and receptivity of the individual. Yet the response should be as general and Universal and as Sheer, just as the origin of that which requires the response is Unique, Universal and Sheer. Those who can so respond, and only the perfect servant of that Sheer Beauty can respond in that way, is where the mystery of Union resides, since this service is the most sublime service, simply because man can do this merely in reflection, and 'one moment of reflection is equal to 70,000 years of devotional prayer'. The short conclusion of this is the test of one's receptivity, one's concordance with the Divine Plan and one's acceptance of unconditional service to that Sheerness and one's ability to do so.

If one asks oneself, 'Am I capable of this?', the answer is general and universal. There is no man who is in the image of He who has fashioned man in His own image who has not been given, in potential, that ability. What then hinders each or any, is the choice so to do or not, or, in other words, the resolve so to serve or not, without in that service there being any odour of an intention of serving oneself even marginally or accidentally. Finally, all depends on the individuated individual.

'That which Is, always Is ...'

THAT which Is, always Is. It is now as It always was and always will be – for It there is no Past other than the Past Present and no Future other than the Present Future. In It there is no change, there is only becoming. At every instant It is in a different configuration. All Its configurations are Its own potential and possibilities co-existent in It with Itself. For It there is neither a new becoming nor an old becoming. All Its becomings are Its own modes of that which Is. Other than It there is no other. It is the Only, the Unique. To It is all Grace and Gratitude.

'What is the single most important point ...'

WHAT is the single most important point that must be understood by a person who wants to know?

It is that there is only One, Unique, Absolute, Infinite Existence. It must be more than an idea. One has to be so completely certain of it that one adopts it through reason and intuition as the basic unshakeable fact of one's existence.

When it is like that in one's existence, then every possible ramification that occurs to one is seen as not being outside The Existence, but as being an aspect of it.

Accept and completely adopt the idea that there is only the Unique, Absolute Existence, apart from which there is not. Then constantly, or as much as possible, keep it in mind. Then, as only He can adopt such an idea, you disappear in the face of the awareness of this idea (which is Him in any case – who else could think of It?). Then your consciousness of this idea is your consciousness of His Existence; His consciousness of Himself. Then where are you? You never were.

He shows you He is yourself, then bit by bit He shows you how He is all that there is. These showings are His caprices, until all exterior existence is known as Him. He shows you He is you, then shows you (Himself) that all else is Him.

In the instant, all so-called progress is annihilated in Him.

TRANSLATIONS

God also has
a name which is *Hū*

*Translation from a pamphlet in Turkish written by the son
of a close friend and pupil of Hasan Shushud Konevi.*

GOD also has a name which is *Hū*. The name *Hū* is indicative of
Singleness of Source, (or singleness of potentiality). Whereas
the name 'God' is indicative only of singleness of Plurality.
Because the level (degree, state, or rung) of Divinity, that is the
level of Godhead, is a level of Divinity which includes all the
knowable pluralities and the external pluralities wherein this
Divinity resides. Thus the name 'God' and He who is at the level
of Godhead, has encompassed all the knowable pluralities
known to the Prime Intellect of God, as well as all the external
pluralities, including the sum total of all the names and attributes of all existents (being), and all the creatures (the creation)
in this world and the next, and specifically whatever there is of
plurality, and has gathered it all within Himself.

The name *Hū* is the passage of the Absolute Being from the
state of *'amā'* (non-manifestation) to the state of Self-cognosis,
which is the level of the Singularity of Potential (or Source).
There is no higher level than this.

Extract from the
Teachings of Osman Fazli

*Extract from the teaching of Osman Fazli of the Jaluti sect;
educator, initiator, teacher and friend of Ismail Hakki Bursevi.*

MAN does not possess anything else but his sensibilities as his real organ of intelligence, and without Divine action man cannot even use his memory which is his sacred treasury of experience acquired long ago. The initiate, the saint, *insān al-kāmil*, is he who possesses the faculty of being able to recognise the true non-existence of his faculties of thought and his own impotence in putting them in motion. It is he who leaves all the 'space' to God and who passes all his life in controlling his intimate faithfulness, in actions, 'thoughts' or in the acts that materialise them. It is he who prays constantly to God, even if it be only by a breath or by a movement of the heart, when he perceives the natural and constant phenomena of thought. In fact everybody knows that this faculty is permanent, constant, irresistibly active. The intimate work of the mystic consists, therefore in trying to attain the Divine proximity, to respond to His infinite clemence by his recognition, or through *zikr*, whenever thoughts, 'visitors from heaven', manifest in his interior. Good or tempting, these visitors have for their mission the exercising of our discernment to the most subtle degree of 'Good and Evil', whereby we accord them our consent or we refuse them.

The Hidden Treasure
(*Kenz-i-Mahfi*)

A translation from the writings of Ismail Hakki Bursevi.

Now ... Qualities, from the faces of actions ... Names from the mirror of Qualities ... Ipseity from the veil of Names are looked at ... and ... man has no strength to climb beyond this ... because that place is the Ipseity; it is the Universe of perplexity and awe ... unless there be a flash of revelation from that place to the Complete Saint (*Walī*). That is to say that there be reflected a light from the Light of Ipseity ... and this also is instantaneous; this can only happen in an instant as short as the blinking of an eye ... and this is why it is called flash. Just as, if the flash of lightning (were) durated any length of time it would blind the eye, this revelation would in the same way blind 'vision' (*baṣīrat*). It is because of this, that most of the Divine Revelations are from behind the veil, because the degree of possibility (*imkān*) cannot withstand the purity of the degree of necessarily so-ness (*wujūb*), and this is no matter how the heart of the Perfect Man is the abode of the *Raḥmān* and the point of reflection of the Divine Vision. What is also so, is that this can only happen according to his ability to receive (*istiʿdād*), and this is known by those who know.

ON IBN ʿARABĪ

Concerning the
Kernel of the Kernel

MUḤYĪDDĪN Ibn 'Arabī is known as the *Shaykh al-Akbar*, the greatest of all Shaykhs, not only for the quantity of his writings, but also for the quality of his exposition as a teacher of the ways and means by which the student of metaphysics may arrive at a higher level of gnosticism. In all Sufi tradition, the aim is the development of man, step by step, until he reaches a point of *ma'ārifa* (Divine Knowledge) where he is known as the *'ārif* (the knower). Being an *'ārif* is not an aim in itself since the real Sufi aim is union, and through the way that the *'ārif* will take in his further ascension and development he will approach his aim. This he does through a process of ripening, not only though introspection, but also by a study of the origin of his self: he is likened to the fruit which must search in its own kernel for the cause and the possibility of its ripening. Ibn 'Arabī's *Kernel of the Kernel* is an invaluable clarification of stages of progress, not for just anyone, but more for the *'ārif* who is in search of the structure of this kernel.

Ibn 'Arabī's works are innumerable – well over three hundred. He often wrote what we might call pamphlets dealing with one or the other of the important questions which needed elucidation or confirmation in detail. This short work of Ibn 'Arabī's is not one of those, nor is it a discussion of any lay interest or curiosity; in fact, it is a dialogue with a mystic/gnostic (*'ārif*) who is ready to look further into the depth of his own interior, to the kernel of the kernel which is his essence. It is not a lightly conversational discussion where weighty matters are implied or

21

hinted at, but a definite assertion and directive as to how this kernel, once found within one, is to be understood and tasted if one wishes to arrive at a higher level of mystical intuition. Since all aim of gnosticism is the perfection of man, in this book Ibn 'Arabī gives a qualitative, recognisable delineation of what it takes to perfect oneself, to become fully matured and emerge in the man-God image.

However, for the final stages of union, the applicant must possess different levels of understanding, of which Ibn 'Arabī speaks but cannot explain 'in words or writing, because it is not permitted'. This short work of Ibn 'Arabī's, one of his most important writings, is a book addressed to the gnostic wherein is described authoritatively and very directly what Philo of Alexandria refers to as: 'the Perfect Man is God, but not The God'.

Ibn 'Arabī's 'metaphysics' are entirely based on the simple factor of the Unity of Existence, which means not that a plurality is unified in Oneness, but that there is nothing else or other than that Only One and Unique Existent, wherein the plurality is a relativisation of the Absolute Oneness – looked at from the uniqueness towards multiplicity – corroborating in the twelfth century AD, though in reverse, the theory of the twentieth century Einstein, where everything is relative, one to another, but curiously, *ad infinitum.*

Only if the reader keeps in mind the essential premise of Ibn 'Arabī's metaphysics, the Unity of Existence (*waḥdat al-wujūd*) which he discusses more fully in his *Risālat al-Wujūdiya* (Treatise on Being)[1] can one fully appreciate the intricacies and depth of the *ma'ārifa* necessary for the complete and clear vision of the devolution of the absolute uniqueness of the Ipseity to the multiplicity of immanence. In short, it is like a grand staircase thrown down from above at man's feet, and where the man

1. Published as *Whoso Knoweth Himself.* Translated by T. H. Weir. Beshara Publications, 1976; reprinted 1988.

stands ready to ascend towards his origin and his essence armed with nothing more than veracity and resolution. In this translation, which keeps to the original text as best it can, several passages may seem inadequate, leaving suggestions without satisfactory elaboration. Most of this is due to Ibn 'Arabī's way of expression in writing, since his ideal is the *jawāmi' al-kalīm* (a few words collected together to explain a lot of things). In other words, even in Ibn 'Arabī's Arabic writings, certain passages are intentionally made to seem obscure, so that the reader may learn to read the proper meaning according to his own aptitude into the collection of words which form these sentences. It is not the intention of this translation to guide or in any way colour the private and personal understanding of the reader. Consequently, this translation conforms as much as possible, not only to the literal meaning of Ibn 'Arabī's exposition, but also to the spirit of his writing. It scrupulously avoids any interference in the personal understanding of the reader. Any explanation and explanatory footnotes are therefore meticulously avoided. It is towards the assurance of this purpose that the translation was submitted to a number of collaborators for correction and elimination of any influences derivable from the construction of a sentence or the usage of a word. In short, the translation presents itself to the reader as the kernel of Ibn 'Arabī's *Kernel of the Kernel*.

All that remains, then, is to re-affirm the gratitude the translator has to Ibn 'Arabī (may God preserve his secret) himself, and also to the great saint and *quṭb* of his time, Ismail Hakki Bursevi (may God preserve his secret), the head of the Jeluti order of Sufis, for the Turkish annotations and translation of the original text. May God lead us all.

The 'Kernel of the Kernel' was published by
Beshara Publications in 1981, and reprinted 1997.

Introduction to the
Fuṣūṣ al-Hikam

DUE to the wealth of detail and elaborate attention to the
proper exposition of what for him are facts which he has
proven, so to speak, before our eyes, Ibn 'Arabi's tenet presents
a complete, circular and magnificent system of perfect Oneness, where all the questions that are sometimes left only partially explained, here find satisfactory answers from both
religious and philosophical approaches. He affirms that "there
is nothing but God". Not only that He is everything, and that
"like unto Whom there is nothing", but also that He is not just
a conglomeration of everything there is, on the contrary, but
that there is nothing other than Him even though everything is
not Him. He manifests Himself in an infinity of forms. God
does not contain, but is, all the forms, and yet He has no form.
He is the essence of all existence. Hence man's existence can
only be through Him. Looked at, then, from man's point of
view, there is beyond man and inclusive of himself, One Reality, One Essence and One Existence, of which man partakes, to
which man relates, in which man finds his own Reality and
relationship. Since, as we have seen, that there is no other existent but the One and Only and Unique Existent, the Reality of
the universes is again the same as that of man. The difference
between man and the universe, of which he is obviously a part,
is therefore only a difference in the concentration of consciousness. To this consciousness it is the mystic's heart alone which
is most fully receptive.

Divine Essence is unqualifiable. It is endowed with Attributes only when It manifests Itself, and consequently all created things are the result of His Attributes. His Attributes are identical with Himself. When viewed apart from Him they are nothing. Since the universe, and everything in it, is the consequence of God's manifested Attributes, its existence is relative; God alone is Absolute. The Divine Essence is the knower, the known and the knowing, and since there exists no other than Him there exists a complete unity of subject, object and the relationship between them.

Where everything devolves from the One and Only Source, the Essence, there can be no question of a creation – a situation when there was not and then there was. Creation *ex nihilo*, then, is unimaginable. Also, nothing cannot produce something. Since there was no time when there was not, and the universe was not created at some time in the past, then it must be that it manifests constantly the Divine Existence. It can be said that the universe is in a perpetual state of recreation out of time, creation meaning simply the coming into concrete manifestation of something already existing. It is the causes within the thing itself which result in that thing coming into manifestation, albeit according to the Divine plan. This is not a plan as an object, but rather the plan of His Own Being and consequential and subsequent manifestation. God has only to will it – to say "Be" – for it to happen. That which qualifies what has thus come to be is the Divine Attribute. A Divine Attribute is a Divine Name manifested in the external world. The Divine Essence is unqualifiable and embraces both Its own non-phenomenal and phenomenal aspects. These manifestations are particular aspects of Reality.

It follows that the Divine consciousness must embrace all the intelligible forms of the prototypes or *a'yān*. Consequently, the Divine Essence embraces all the potential essences of the prototypes. In fact these potentialities are the 'latent realities' or *a'yān al-thabita*. The Essence of each of these then is no other than a 'mode' of God.

26

These latent realities or potentialities which are of and in the Essence, present in the unqualifiable Existent, never get manifested. It is the images of their potentialities which are the manifested 'modes'. All the seemingly existent multitude of things and beings are therefore, as images of the *a'yān,* individuated 'modes' of His Existence. It is this multitude of individuated 'modes' of the Essence which form the phenomenal aspects of the One and Only Reality. Therefore the phenomenal world is a reality in its Essence by virtue of the whole of this manifestation, which is no other than the particular aspects of Reality qualified and thereby rendered relative, and only the relative image of the unlimited and infinite potentialities which is the unqualifiable Divine Essence.

The 'mechanism' of manifestation on the other hand is at once simple, since it is an expression of the Divine Will – Be – and complex, due to the nature of the variable and infinite relativities expressed as the phenomenal universe. The basic factor of this manifestation into relativity, however, is still the Divine Essence as One. But equally one must bear in mind that there must be a parallel to this, a manifestation of the One Absolute and Unqualifiable as the Qualifiable One, an equally valid manifestation of the Essence of the One, again, into a qualifiable multiplicity – the whole process remaining as The One and The Unique at the same time. Consequently, the only manner in which this can happen, is for the Unique Unqualifiable Essence to express Itself, to exteriorise Itself as a multiplicity – remaining the Unique Unqualifiable Essence as the interior Reality of this expression. We have, then, a curious seeming duality of the exteriorised Uniqueness as a multiplicity of images and forms and, at the same time, we have the Unique Unqualifiable Essence manifested *in toto* in all Its qualities and attributes. The former Ibn 'Arabi calls the Perfect Man, the latter the Godhead. The qualifiable multiplicity of the One, known as God or the Godhead, is no other than the multiplicity of the Divine Names and Attributes.

There is no state higher than a man can reach – higher even than the angels and archangels, and this is obviously due to the fact that though angels and archangels and other such phenomenal modes of expression of the Unique Essence are limited modes of His individuation, the nature of the Perfect Man remains, and equally retains, the original, essential, unlimited, therefore unqualifiable potentialities of the Essence. It is because of this difference among all that we call creation, that [man is] the only exteriorisation of the Divine Essence which, though it is manifest as an individuation, also retains in its interior all the potentialities of the Essence. Therefore, the individual man, from among all that is known as creation, is the only one upon whom it is incumbent and for whom it is possible, to acquire knowledge and in a way to re-ascend to a close relationship, and a realisation, a 'union' or 're-union' with his origin. When this happens, and only then, is man conscious, and only the heart of the mystic can fully receive this consciousness. Thereby God manifests in individuations and modes, in attributes and qualities for the completion of His Self Expression as the conscious man fulfils this expression by the cognisance of his Reality, like the joining of the end of the circle to its beginning.

Now, this circular and complete movement has as cause only one factor. That factor is Love. That is why the *ḥadīth qudsī* which says, "I was a Hidden Treasure and I loved to be known..." retains such an eminent position in Ibn 'Arabi's and all other mystical lore. It is then obvious that the prime motive of this circular movement is nothing other than Love, which finds its object in its self-projection and the return of this projection to its Reality. It is because of this that man says, "He is me. I am no other than Him, though I am not Him."

Universality and Ibn 'Arabī

A vision which comprises a whole with all its possible ramifications is a universal perception. Ibn 'Arabī's perception of the Unity of Existence is of that sort of existence where the One and Only Existence includes and comprises a whole with all its ramifications. If one looked at a pyramid from the point of view of its apex which bears the Ben-Ben stone of the ancient Egyptian theology as its real purpose of existence, and saw its constructional and other complexities as the ramifications of this one point and purpose, one would approach the stand-point of view of Ibn 'Arabī and his vision of the Universes, which for 'convenience' he prescribes 18,000 – though 'they are endless in number'.

Ibn 'Arabī looks at these universes like a man in a helicopter poised over the apex of the pyramid, looking at the pyramid as an expression of one singular purpose, its existence explained by the uniqueness of the apex with all the ramifications of its stable proposition and plane of construction, etc., etc., following from that purpose.

Ibn 'Arabī's conception of the Unity of Existence is that there is a Unique Existence with Universal ramifications. He has not in mind so much an Existent which, for him, as a concept, would limit existence into one conceptual Being, but rather the Existence which at one stage of self-expression poses as an Existent. This is the God-head which comes into being at the second level of the self-expression of the Existence – the second degree of the First *Ta'ayyun*.

Plurality is a latent possibility as a consequence of being the One and the Unique. Thus, the Unity conceptually predicates the plurality. Where Existence as such is Unique, the Existent, equally, contains this latent generality of plurality of the general Existence because the Existence is General and Universal – even though as yet the word Universal has not come into being and acquired a meaning. This Universality, again, is latently present in the Concept of an Existent which although necessarily one as an Existent, is universal, general and all-encompassing since it is not other than The Existence. It is this concept of a Unique, all-pervading Existence which is not limited in any way, which is at the centre of Ibn 'Arabī's conceptual Universality of the Divine.

It is a particular attribute of Ibn 'Arabī that for him there has never been an isolation of form or an intellectual entity as a Divinity, be it the Only or Unique Existent. It is all Existence which is represented both as God or the Ipseity of God. Even where he eulogises the Muhammedan way of thought, which is a monotheistic unity, he prefers to explain the Existent's limitlessness by diffusing it into the concept of Existence rather than an Existent, and refers to his explanation as the Muhammedian Way.

It is perhaps his single-pointedness which constitutes Ibn 'Arabī's Universality. At first sight, this may seem like a paradox. However, it is the basis of his stand-point of view which results in this seemingly rigid stand, whence he observes all the extent of possibilities, no matter how relative or absolute, and which takes him into the domain of a boundless Universality.

Another (a second) aspect of Ibn 'Arabī's Universality lies in the fact, for him always true, that everything is an expression of Beauty. Where He is Sheer Beauty, unqualifiable even by the attribute of beauty or beautiful, where man is in the image of this Perfection as the Qur'ānic verset says, 'I have created man in the most beautiful fashion', (ahsan, from the root husn, meaning beauty) and where Nature as such, universal, is no other than the expansion of the Breath of the Compassionate Ipseity (Nafas ar-Rahmān), there can be no attribute to all immanence, as well as transcendence, other than Beauty. Thus Beauty takes on a universality.

This is understandable if, from our point of view, Beauty can and does express itself not in form, but in response to a 'vision' which engenders in us a sentiment, clear, not of murky emotionalism, but a full correspondence to an awe-inspiring wonderment which, in his terminology, is the *jalāl*, the flip-side of *jamāl* (Beauty), where the extreme superlative, the *jamāl*, applies to the state of the Ipseity and thence to God. We have put vision in quotes because this vision is not relegated only to the sensory eye, but to all that evokes a 'taste' (*dhawq*) of gratifying, nevertheless overwhelming, beauty, or beatitude, be it a person, a building, a sunset or a poem, etc., etc.

Whatever the context of the expression of Beauty, the vehicle of Its transport is the sentiment which gives birth, either consciously or unconsciously, or even sub-consciously, to an unrestricted love. This sort of love engulfs the whole being and extends to all existence because where Beauty has moved one into a sentiment of response, that response is similar to the vision of Beatrice on a bridge over the River Arno in Florence which reverberated as the passion aroused in Dante – eternal, universal, all-encompassing. It is this passion which moved Dante to say, 'Love does not excuse the beloved from loving back'. It is this initial love which moves the Ipseity to express Itself at all, which pervades all we call creation, or, in Ibn 'Arabī's terms, self-expression.

This, then, is a further aspect of Ibn 'Arabī's universality in that all is the result, the cause, the effect and the state of love. For Ibn 'Arabī, religion or belief is 'whichever way love's mounts take, that is my religion and my faith'.

Here, then, is a triune existence which forms the unlimitable basis of Ibn 'Arabī's universality. Since no part of this triad of uniqueness of all existence, its state of Sheer Beauty and its expression vehicled by love, can be limited to a form or be contained, encompassed in a non-general or non-universal state,

31

thought, or belief, then one is obliged, in short, to admit a superlative universality where Ibn 'Arabī is concerned.

To go into further exposition or explanation of this would need unlimited pages, hours, words, even a new language where expressions would be non-relative. For the moment then, the astounding Chinese expression of Lao Tzu is enough to point at a universality which, in Japan, Professor Izutsu[1] has managed to show – how closely the two sources of thought, so differently expressed, are nevertheless germane in their universality.

---

1. See *Sufism and Taoism* by Toshihiko Izutsu. University of California Press, 1984.

Wisdom and Wisdoms

EXISTENCE is one and only and unique. The existences of the beings are varied and consequent to the Unique Existence, the Unique Being.

Unicity prescribes total and absolute inclusiveness; thereby bearing the plurality of fruiting in the uniqueness of the seed.

Thus the Unique Existence in its necessary self-consciousness compiles an integration of knowledges which in themselves elucidate discernment and subsequently formulate an advisory sound judgement without a hint of condemnation; this tested against the background of intellect and intuition condescends in mankind as Wisdom.

Man is no other than a mirror image synthesising Being.

The Synthesis of Being is expressed by synchronicity of global influences that rule and set the parameters of a holistic image which is known as 'manifestation'.

This manifestation is the individuation into relative context of that synthesis, while Being remains unassailed and integral as the source from which all expressions of relationships emanate and diversify *ad infinitum*.

Infinity does not propose the three considerations that qualify the relative state. The requisites that render manifestation relative are: Time, Space, Distance. Infinity is not concerned with any of these 'dimensions'. However, it holds relativity within the consequences of its concept, remaining all the while unassailed, like the Being which it qualifies. Here the qualification does not colour the qualified; but the qualified engenders the qualification in consequence of self expression which remains subsequent and not integral.

This is prevalent in all circumstances of relationships without ever attaining the Being, which always remains, untouched by its qualities; unqualifiable. What remains unqualifiable remains unknowable, except in its effects, because expression and expressing is qualification. The awesome knowledge of this and its consequences of veridic and verified judgement appertains to Wisdom. When this is given to whomsoever 'great good is established'.

With Ibn 'Arabī, wisdom becomes qualifications of the Ipseity in manifestation. Individuations bear these qualifications in total expression of their own temporal selves. These are the *Ḥikam*, the Wisdoms that perform the devolvement from gem to setting to satisfy the perfection of the jewel. Although *Ḥikma* is its qualification, Being still remains unlimited and unaffected by it, for the sheer reason that It Itself emanates the qualification in manifestation which is no more than the mere effect of Its infinite possibilities, while Itself remains far beyond any qualification as such.

The personifications of the individualised Wisdoms appear periodically through time as the era requires their presence to achieve completion. But these personifications, the *Ḥikam* (Wisdoms) are no other than the global holistic images of the synthesis of the Being, reflecting in relative exposure, aspects of the whole.

Take for instance the *Ḥikma* (Wisdom) of *Raḥmāniya* (Compassionateness) in the Word of Solomon. One reads at the end of the chapter on Solomon in the *Fuṣūṣ al-Ḥikam*:

'If we exposed to thee the spiritual state of Solomon in all its plenitude, thou wouldst be struck with terror. The majority of the wise men of this spiritual way are ignorant of the true state of Solomon and his rank; the reality is not that which they suppose'.[1]

1. From *The Wisdom of the Prophets* translated by Titus Burckhardt/Angela Culme-Seymour. Beshara Publications, Gloucestershire, 1975.

What has been perceived of Solomon in relative exposure is only an aspect of the holistic image of the *Raḥmān* (The Compassionate).

God says: 'Call me God (*Allāh*), call me The Most Compassionate (*Raḥmān*) ...' Then, those with perfect perception should undoubtedly see the holistic image of *Allāh* when they see the *Raḥmān*. However, under the influence of the relative state of vision, the hologram image of *Raḥmān* is only restrictedly aspected into perception, giving rise to the quote at the end of the chapter on Solomon: 'If we exposed to thee the spiritual state of Solomon in all its plenitude ...'

What Ibn 'Arabī refers to in this sentence is the holistic image perception of the *Raḥmān*, which he refrains from exposing. This image would definitely be in conjugation with *Allāh*, and would consequently be terrifying to perceive since it would hold in one instant through infinity all opposition and proposition at once. This would be impossible to relate to for a rational relative intellect. All the Bounteous Compassion, as a free gift, would deluge fittingly, proportioned and limitless, upon the man, not as in unloading from one and loading onto the other, but as the Being of endlessly Bounteous Compassion devolving through the Being in Its aspect as Solomon the Man. This would be impossible to bring into any metaphysical or perceptual coincidence with any intellectual aspiration, no matter how wild and widely hyperbolic and imaginative. This is what remains esoteric; and what we find exoteric in Solomon is what the *Raḥmāniya* gives as effect (as related by Ibn 'Arabī), considered as sufficient material to understand the magnitude of *Raḥmān* and the free gift that devolves from it. Hence our limitation brings into being the often quoted sentence: 'The beginning of Wisdom is fear of God', for the easy use by the many.

Personified Wisdoms, the *Ḥikam*, are intellectualised, direct expressions of potential represented as fixed possibilities in the inexpressed thought realisations or mentations of the Being.

35

At this juncture these expressions cannot be, as yet, qualified as an expression, simply because they have not as yet devolved into the exterior, either as vision or as sound.

Now, if we remember the importance Ibn 'Arabī attaches to sound as primordial expression of will and how, consequently, 'things' are effected and affected and influenced by even a letter – like the letter waw [2] for instance, or by the syllable full of consequence, *Kun*, be – then we will arrive unavoidably at the point where an auditory impulsion received and accepted is certainly the most effective, if not the major consequential expressive impulse as such. This combines both the elements of order (*Ḥukm*, from the same root as *Ḥikma*) as well as the necessary auditory reaction – a point which again, Ibn 'Arabī strongly underlines as the only possible acceptable correlative of sound – the hearing and listening.

However, hearing and listening do not always reverberate the same intensity of motive or concordance; one, sometimes, remaining completely passive, whereas the other may be simply active enough to be receptive but with no consequential 'motor' reaction to corroborate an active acceptance with subsequent concordance. To these two may be added a further two, one of which will be a submissive reaction culminating in concordant action; or the reverse which is 'rebellion' and its varied and multitudinous reactions. But these last two modes are not the limits of our exposition. It is necessary, therefore, to define the limits of *Ḥikma* (Wisdom) to the action of pronouncement, otherwise known as 'invitation', to the pronouncement – ('You are only sent to invite' – *Qur'ān*) – because Wisdom does not coerce in any way except by exposition of Truth and its modal applicability to the space-time defined state; or even to the statement, relevant.

2. See *Mystical Astrology According to Ibn 'Arabī* by Titus Burckhardt, translated by Bülent Rauf. Beshara Publications, 1977; reprinted 1989.

This is exactly the mode of action of Essential Devolvement through an erstwhile mentation where a state of self-awareness engenders self-existence as its natural consequence, but without a cause and effect procession or any lateral or perpendicular time relationship. There is only a *de facto* statement manifesting in exposition as wisdom – given, where 'given' only refers to the ability in the subject receiving the gift to perceive that which is proffered, and more intensely, to recognise it as what it is meant to be, with all the appertaining intrinsic and extrinsic consequential activity of complete and absolute vision and equally, complete inaction. ('The Wise man does not act' – Lao Tsu).

Yet we should note that the action of the name does not make the person performing the action, the actor. It is rather the meaning of the action which identifies with the man who is performing the action. The Wise is such a name and Wisdom, as we have seen, is the identity of the man through whom Wisdom is promulgated.

All the Words who are Wisdoms defile through our conceptual time, sometimes in accordance with our temporal procedure and sometimes metachronically, till a consequence of complete exposition of the non-coercive judgement in accordance with Essential knowledge is reached.

Ibn 'Arabī adhibits these Wisdoms, each, as emanating from the Words. But this does not eliminate the blatancy of the incorporation of Wisdom into the Word and their conjunction. The sound of the Word reaches intelligible response in the manifested world as the condescension of Wisdom with man at the right instant, since Wisdom is consequential to absolute knowledge and therefore not otherwise *qadīm*, or ancient, to the Ipseity since it defines: but it is so to the effect of the Essence in proper proportion and appropriate instance.

Significantly, although beyond the context of this paper, the series of Wisdoms that come down to Muḥammed end with this Seal of Prophethood where a proposal of religious law is concerned. Yet the Word is permanent and cannot end. To this effect, Ibn 'Arabī and all followers of the same way concur that law-giving Prophethood is sealed: but the other kind, the one that does not propose a new religion and religious law, carries on the necessary continuity of the Word and consequently the Wisdom that the Word holds.

Thus it is that the *Fuṣūṣ al-Ḥikam* comes to be put into the hands of Ibn 'Arabī to be exposed as 'people will benefit'; and equally, thus it is that Wisdom is never acquired but always received when given to whom God may choose to give, and once given, to whomsoever, 'great good is established'.

Concerning the
Universality of Ibn 'Arabī

THERE is only one Existence. That existence is, naturally, a state of Being. That Being, then, is the One and Only, Infinite Being. It exists through its own existence irrespective of any other consideration. Naturally so, because there is no other premise than its own existence, therefore there is no other point of reference or relationship in respect of which it could be considered. When it is self-conscious it creates or constitutes its own consideration of itself. This bringing into consciousness of itself as a mentation of its own potential existence is when it 'manifests' itself to itself. This is the only state of its own duality possible or imaginable where the duality is really no other than itself with its own image of itself. This self consciousness of its own mentation of its potentiality takes itself from its own singularity and uniqueness to its own duality of unique singularity only in its own consciousness. At this point of its singularity of duality it is necessary to give existence to all of its own potentialities since these potentialities are of the 'fabric' of its own self-consciousness. These infinite number of potentialities which thus have come to and have acquired existence through the self-consciousness of the essentially self existing Unique, One and Only, Infinite Existence, then, is the only source of number and, consequently, of all possible plurality.

Universality presumes a locus or a multiplicity of areas, a plurality of loci. This plurality, in reference to the One and Only and Infinite Existence, must either deny it or allow a situation where plurality of the One is essentially a self-corporate mode of a many-faceted existence where 'each' individual existence is a consideration of accommodation for this global Uniqueness in expression. Consequently, here the infinity of the One permeates the theoretically many facets of the global one. The result is One expressed manifoldly. Each of these manifoldly expressed facets of the One Infinite Existence are so many Universes all enclosed in the One and Unique Infinite Existent.

People who have been self-styled archi-erudites, motivated by a leaning towards 'byzantinism' and who have thus achieved a chair in the society of the *cymini sectores*, cannot coincide with Ibn 'Arabī's horizon which remains an unlimited, infinite universal vision simply because in Ibn 'Arabī universality is expressed by the infinity contained in the Essential Uniqueness. Here the word 'contained' misrepresents a state where nothing is 'contained' since to 'contain' requires a container which contains by the limits of its own structure. The Essential State has no such limits. Hence to qualify its own Infinity as being 'contained' may lead to a misrepresentation of the Essential State of Being of the Uniqueness. This *sui generis* essentiality qualifies itself by Its Uniqueness which naturally presumes unlimited, therefore Infinite, possibilities which are impossible of number. Incidentally, it could be said that Its 'numerality' is only a conceptual consequence of the triplicity of its being Essential, Infinite, and Unique.

The juxtaposition of Uniqueness and Infinity are, somewhat, complimentaries that form the Essentiality of its Latitude of Being. It is this Being which is expressed through its phase of Infinity that gives rise to our concept of a state of being universal. Then again Ibn 'Arabī underlines the infinite number of these universes ('*awālim*) which according to him may be of the number of the grains of sand on the beach or more, and which, for convenience, he refers to as the Eighteen Thousand Universes.

This cosmology, so to speak, of Ibn 'Arabī is in complete concordance with illumination received by him from the

40

Qur'ān, which Ibn 'Arabī follows assiduously, without ever deviating, even when scholars and 'doctors' find divergence in the words of Ibn 'Arabī from the practice of the Muḥammedan religion, thus 'missing' the depth of the Muḥammedian Way.

A passage of the *Qur'ān* which reflects the infinite plurality of the universes says, 'Lord of the Heavens and of the Earth, Lord of the Universes' (*Rabb as-samawāti w'al-arḍ, Rabb al-'alamīn*). The mention of the second Lordship is not only a poetical adornment in the sentence. It is a pointer to the fact that even though the 'Heavens' (*as-samawāti*) are mentioned in plural, there is still room to draw the attention to the infinite existence of universes (*'alamīn, 'awālim*) beyond our concept of the 'Heavens'. It is the infinity of the Universes aspected with the Lordship and for every potentiality and possibility, beyond the concept of number as we understand it, which qualifies the Esoteric Lordship represented in the Reality of Muḥammed, the Reality of Realities or the Reality of the Muḥammedian Way, by which is meant the esoteric reality of the Muḥammedian meaning – a meaning that Ibn 'Arabī represents himself as the total heir and as the explicit and the implicit attributions of exposed and esoteric meanings involved in the divergent Unicity of the micro- and macro-cosmic Reality of Realities.

In that case, the existence of Ibn 'Arabī himself is the attribution of Reality in the sense of the exposed meaning and the esoteric meaning hermeticized in the cosmos both as macro- and micro-, where these two are inconsequentially equal before the Reality of Unique, Infinite, Essentiality.

This is the basis of the all-important 'Universality' of Ibn 'Arabī.

ARTICLES AND INTERVIEWS

Union

*Paper given to the World Symposium
on Humanity, London, 1979.*

It is indeed a pleasure for us of Beshara to talk of Union. This is our daily bread and meat since our constant and only aim is to reach that point in the Unity of Existence which we call Union. Consequently, we greet with joy everyone who is sincerely concerned with Union and who wants to promote or establish in this world that Union which is the sole purpose, and the only reason, for man on earth.

We ardently believe that there is Only One Indivisible and Unique Existent, and to keep it simple, all the multitude we seem to see is nothing other than the image in relativity of the One Absolute and Complete Being. This is what we call the Unity of Existence.

For centuries, man has known, spoken, insisted on this Truth from one end of the world to the other. All whom we know in our common history of mankind as wise men, as prophets, sages etc. have repeated in different languages this same universal Reality. All religions from the most ancient to the most recent have built their esoteric foundations on the same fundamental Truth which is the Existence of that Unique Being which is the Absolute Ipseity of what we call *Tao, God, Eluhim, Allāh*, etc., etc.

There is in every man a private place in that Ipseity. He who knows his own reality knows his place in the Ipseity. Through Service, Knowledge and Love we strive for the perfectibility of man. The Perfected Man is in Union with the Ipseity. Philo of

Alexandria, roughly the contemporary of Jesus Christ, wrote: 'The Perfect Man is *Theos* (God) though he is not *'o Theos* (The God)'. Man is not other than his reality, though he is not the Reality.

It is in every man to strive to reach consciousness of this magnitude. When he consciously reaches it, he is in Union with his Essence which is the Ipseity.

For man to be conscious of this possibility, he has only to look around him. It is he alone of all creatures on this earth who can encompass the ideas, make those ideas his own, and call them his facts.

On these facts, like Einstein's $E = mc^2$, or the expanding universe, with all its quasars, pulsars, black holes, or nebulae and galaxies etc., he will encompass other equally staggering facts on which to build further worlds. Surely, with such potential, as Ṣūfis have sometimes said, he is the macrocosm, and that which he encompasses with his mind, the Universe, is the microcosm.

Surely it is true that God has made man in his own Image. With such potential, such capacity to circumscribe and encompass universes in his mind, with his ability to reach Union with the Absolute and thereby Unique Being, than which he is no other, surely man is of a superlative magnitude. No other can reach the development and height that man can reach. If man keeps this reality of his magnitude constantly in his consciousness, that man is a perfect Man. And it is for this Perfect Man that the Universe, which contains his earth, was at all created, so that he can know it, serve it, and love it.

Love is the movement of Beauty. Beauty is the ultimate aim of Love. Where there is no Beauty, there is misery. When the Tibetan Lama Akon came to lecture at our school three to four years ago, one of my co-students asked him why there was so much misery in the world. Akon's answer was as superb as his wisdom. He said, 'Why is there I?' The first person singular. The man whose centre is in his first person singular can neither know nor serve, nor can he love. To arrive at Union man must love. If not, then not. If a man's creed is Love he will crave for, strive for, work for and attain Union.

I quote from a twelfth century mystic from Andalusia, Muḥyīddīn Ibn ʿArabī:

> ... O marvel! a garden amidst flames!
> My heart has become capable of every form: it is a
>   pasture for gazelles and a convent for Christian monks,
> And a temple for idols and the pilgrim's *Kaʿba* and the
>   tables of the *Tora* and the book of the *Koran*.
> I follow the religion of Love: whatever way Love's
>   mounts take,
> that is my religion and my faith.[1]

---

1. From the translation of *The Tarjumān al-Ashwāq* by R. A. Nicholson. Theosophical Publishing House, London, 1911; reprinted 1978.

The Nature of Service

*Extracts from an interview given on
KPFA Radio, California in 1980/1.*

Participants: Will Nofke and Maggie Kurzman of KPFA,
Bülent Rauf and Hugh Tollemache.

WN Welcome to New Horizons. This is Will Nofke and
Maggie Kurzman. Today our guests are members of the
Beshara Foundation in England, Bülent Rauf and Hugh
Tollemache, who are both study guides at the Beshara
School at Sherborne House.

We describe our program as being 'to know, to love
and to serve the universe', and it's the latter that we would
like to concentrate on today: the aspect of service, and
what the true meaning of service is. I think there are a
great many misconceptions about how we can serve one
another and the universe. Bülent, perhaps you could give
us your view of what service – profound service – is.

BR Real service is without the self being self-indulgent in serving people. It has to be completely without the mixation
of the person into the service rendered. There was an example we used to use: if you find, in a very bad situation,
a friend who needs a glass of water and you give him a
glass of water, that's not service; that is friendship. But if
your enemy is on the ground and begs for a glass of
water, and even before he begs you give him a glass of
water: that is service.

WN So it's sensing that the need is there?

BR Yes, the need is always there. Because, if we go deeper into the matter of service, we find that service is not one of the attributes of the Absolute Essence. It's the reverse of service, the Lordship, which is an attribute of the Divine Essence and therefore service, the best service, is only possible if you can identify with the Lord. In the same way, service is a self-identification – without the self interfering in it – with the object that has to be served.

WN When we speak of Lord, we're not speaking in the religious sense necessarily but of he who is to be served, of the person who is to be served?

BR Yes, exactly.

HT I'd like to add a little bit to what Bülent has said. I think a lot of people when they hear the word service consider it to be a facet of do-gooding – something you do really for your own sake and under your own conditions. One really has to go further than that, to the aspect of knowing what it is you are being of service to. People often feel that emotion or love is enough, but it's not.

MK Many people in the act of do-gooding seem to be so caught up in the emotions of doing that I really question how they can remain objective enough to realise that in fact it's not true service.

HT Only through knowledge. To give an example – a very mundane example – a person has a flower in his house, a potted plant. Now, its not enough to water this plant just so that you can appreciate the beauty of the flower. You have to water it because that is what the flower needs for itself and for its self-fulfilment. In this case, you're not imposing on that flower what you want from it, you're giving it what it needs for its own being. This is the same with anything; flower, mineral, animal, human – you serve because of what you can give towards its fulfilment.

50

MK And not just strictly for the feeling of reward within yourself.

HT Yes, exactly, it's not just for the sense of personal satisfaction.

WN One can extend that metaphor in all sorts of ways. In
our anxiety and our desire for a perfect bloom we can
over-fertilise or over-water. In the same way, it's possible
to over-serve a cause by the imposition of our own will.
The implication seems to be, that if one is to do service,
there needs to be a certain familiarity with the so-called
problems that exist – and I'm thinking of social and
political problems. And beyond that: after you're steeped
in the 'facts', you then have to intuitively feel what needs
to be done – anticipate what needs to be done. Bülent, I
wonder if this makes sense to you.

BR It does perfectly because there is no difference between a
servant and a Lord. And if the intuition doesn't come in
at the right point in the servant, he will never know what
the Lord requires him to do. He can reason it out, but that
is not enough. Reason and intuition must go hand in hand
and the result of that must be checked again against reason, and if that is valid, then that is the action to follow.
Otherwise, it's like feeling about in the dark.

   That's why Hugh brought in this lack of knowledge.
All this possibility of reasoning is built on facts acquired
already, which formulate the process of reasoning so that
it is appropriate to the action. If one doesn't know anything about the subject that one is dealing with, it isn't
service. Here is a man hungry and you prepare a bath for
him. That's no good. You must know. Knowledge, therefore study (which goes with knowledge), is essential, and
knowledge and the knower and the known are identical.
Therefore without knowledge there is no possibility of
action – valid action – at all. And service emanates from
there and the result is a sort of self-development of awareness, constant awareness. That's why we say that it's the

51

constancy of the awareness by which a man's spiritual growth is judged: the constancy, not the quantity. That's the training required.

WN That sounds like quite a training process.

BR Indeed it is.

WN You managed to sneak in something there that could be the subject of an entire program – the knowledge, the knower and the known being one. I believe that this is important, because if one is not truly aware and has no sense of the unity of existence and the servant and the person served being of one essence, then you can actually do disservice out of a lack of empathy with the person that you're serving. Say someone is hungry and you see there is hunger there, and you force-feed them, regardless of their ability to receive the food; this is disservice.

BR This is quite true. This is why at the Beshara Schools we have no teachers. Because a teacher will set out a schedule of study and will keep you to it whether you are able to resist the weight of it or not. Whereas if you have the study group itself arranging and limiting itself to what it can absorb, and you sit there with them to see that they have done that before they go further, then you are not force-feeding them.

MK I've heard various teachers talk about service in terms of giving their 'students' some discipline or obedience towards themselves. In other words, serving the teacher is a way of learning how to serve.

BR It must take a great deal of courage for a teacher to differentiate himself from a student. A teacher is also a student. Knowledge belongs to the Knower which is situated, starts from, the premise that there is only One Existent. That One Existent is the Knower and we're all given a portion of knowledge. So none of us can assume superiority of knowledge over another. With students, it's a matter of their time and their development. Today what

52

we call a student may be at a certain point in his capacity to absorb knowledge, but tomorrow he can even surpass the teacher.

WN Looking through the prospectus of the school, and noticing that you study works from many different traditions, it seems to me that the people who undertake this kind of study must already have resolved within themselves the seeming differences in various religious philosophies; that they have come to some understanding already of the Unity of Existence that underlies all of them.

BR The foundation of all religious belief is the same unity. If each student only goes back down within their own religion, they will find that. Even the Zoroastrian religion, which is built to all outward purposes on a duality; if you go beyond the textbooks and look within the people, you will find that the two come out of one. There is no possibility of studying any religion in depth, to the foundation of it, without coming up with that same One Unique Essence. So no matter what religion people come from, or whatever intention they come from, they will have to come sooner or later, if they want to advance esoterically – mystically, religiously, whatever way they want to advance – they will come to that One, Unique Essence in the end anyhow.

I will tell you a story: the Bishop of Gloucester came to visit us one day and he said; 'Where do these people come from? Who are these people?' There was a girl in charge of showing them around and she said, 'These are people who have questioned their existence'. That's all.

MK I sense really a tremendous timeliness in all that's being said and I think that is because there seems to be so much disillusionment today. It seems to come from various sources, one being people who have gone the path of traditional religion and feel that that didn't answer whatever it was they were seeking. And people who have been

53

following teachers, particularly during this last period of say, five or six years, have also become disillusioned.

BR I quite agree with you. Let's take the case of the people being in religion and being disillusioned. Whichever religion they are involved with, they are disillusioned because each religion is like a medieval town. It has a very strong fortress around it: you are either in that town or you're outside of it. Whereas the other people who go in for learning through teachers and things, they submit to a dictatorship with which they will surely, in time, be disillusioned.

WN We've talked now of love, service and the inner life. Now I'd like to throw it open to you to develop anything which you feel is left incomplete.

BR Perhaps when we speak of reason, we need to mention also science, because science and thereby technological advance, which so many people have questioned and criticised, is an integral part of the way this world is moving. Manifestation – all manifestation – does not happen except in the manner of the place of manifestation's movement. This scientific progress and technology as it goes on today is that through which all manifestation, and the further knowledge which we shall acquire, shall come.

WN That's an interesting viewpoint in the light of the fact that science seems to be validating some of the more esoteric things that have been said over the centuries. It's really amusing to watch this; a vast number of people will not accept anything until it's been scientifically proven, and it seems that science is indeed proving these things to the satisfaction of that part of us that demands that sort of proof.

BR Yet you notice that there is nothing unreasonable in science, and all our knowledge is based on reason. Reason is our touchstone as to whether something is acceptable or not, even though it is mixed with intuition. Intuition and reason, weighed against reason again, checked against reason again, is what we go by. And science does the same: science is at the service of reason.

HT I think in the future it must be that religion and science begin to complement each other: that science without religion will find future development extremely difficult. Religion without science equally will come to an impasse because now, what is happening is that what people considered to be miracle in the past is now science.

MK There's something else that comes to my mind and that is that we tend to think of science as discovery. I happened to mail a letter for Will today and on the address it said 'Ancient Future' and it just fascinated me, because I really do see that what we're talking about is really that blend of the ancient with the future.

BR It is definitely for the future. But there is no purpose for an old man at all in this world except helping the future. In the same way, anything that is ancient is at the service of the future. In fact, in reality, there is no such thing as time ...

But going back to what Hugh said about science, he mentioned religion. I would like to call what he calls religion, belief. Because religion to my mind is the set forms of religion which cannot to be tied down into form. The universe is too big to be tied down to one little form. It's infinite.

A Consideration since Assisi

A comment in Beshara Magazine on a meeting between the major faiths and conservationists in Assisi in 1986.

THAT which is already not cannot become that which it is. Is there no development, then, no metamorphosis?

Development is the becoming. One must remember, though, that this is not a process but a realisation. It is when one has realised in oneself, no matter what that self may be, that one is that which it is – then the self has realised its development and its becoming. If the self yearns for completeness then it will realise itself in completeness when it becomes the complete self. If, on the other hand, it is satisfied with an aspect of completeness then it will realise itself only to that extent and will not go further. This is in case it has the desire to go further. The potential exists in every self; the choice is 'personal', individual, sometimes flawed by or encumbered by a lack, a deficient receptivity due to one thing or another of its own choice and/or making, but never essentially.

However, it remains that Nature is the expansion of the breath of the Most Compassionate; therefore it englobes all possibilities inherent in the Essential. To remain in the choice of aspects of this total Compassionate Nature – like interest in Geology, in wildlife, in childcare, in RSPCA work, in Forestry or Fisheries, etc. – is useful in bringing one to the recognition of the Total Essence through particularised media. When the self is fully tuned and is in harmony and has complete knowledge of the Essential factor which permeates Nature, it is impossible for that self to disregard any particularised sector and refrain from putting all its efforts and ability and tact to the service of that which is no other than the closest kin of its own Spirit. Because that self will be constantly aware that the self is a particularisation of the One Universal Self imbued with the Breath which at the same time permeates, and is inherent in, Total Nature of Compassion in the unlimited expanse of, not only this world, but also all the universes.

A self which re-integrates the One and Only Self must perforce be conscious and aware constantly of this integrity, knowing full well that the service of the universes is the service of the Spirit.

Such a man is rare, one might think. But the development of anyone to this degree of consciousness is within at once one's potential and power. Only choice interferes, and the fact that the self has choice is its guard-light to its closeness and intimacy to and with The Spirit.

The choice is a matter of taste. Good taste is learned, there-fore given freely to allow the essential development through the potential of the Self. 'Given' is what is 'learned'. One can only learn what is given, but being given is dependent upon desire to receive for its effect – *potentia oboedientalis*. The resultant 'learning' is a realisation which comes in some linear time after the lesson is learned. This is the usual procedure. A more direct procedure is to submit to a system of receptivity, for instance like in those schools of esoteric education open to all those who wish to imbibe therein, like Beshara – which word is itself a promise, because joy is a resultant and perfect if it is the conse-quence of good taste. In a very remarkable and delightful exposé by Dr Karan Singh which starts with the genius of Rabindranath Tagore, this is aptly put, but we believe that this ideal situation should not be considered a prerequisite for the conservationist. Rather, the conservationist should naturally be in this ideal state if he acquired the necessary learning and taste. However, again, this depends on the individual decision and desire to undergo willingly the servitude of Love and Beauty. This is what Beshara serves. This is what Beshara strives for.

To Suggest a Vernacular ...

A comment in Beshara Magazine concerning
developments in modern science.

In an old article which appeared some time ago under the head-
ing of 'Opinions' entitled 'Quarks, Quasars and The Meaning
of Life' by Paul Davies, it is quoted, presumably from Professor
Davies; 'This theme of simplicity, wholeness and beauty –
revealed through mathematical formulae or delicate experimentation – recurs again and again as nature's mysteries and
subtleties are explored.'

If you leave out that which is between the two dashes, what
Professor Davies marvels at has been expounded upon in
exactly the same tone as the quote above and in much greater
detail and depth seven to eight centuries ago – not to go any
further back in time – by the one who is known as the greatest
of all teachers, Doctor Maximus, or, because he developed in
Moorish Spain and in Arabic, as the Shaykh al-Akbar.[1]

Whether it is the credit of modern physics or not to
rediscover these Essential truisms, well known to many, and
re-express them in modern 'mathematical formulae or delicate
experimentation' is secondary to the immanence of the context
of appreciation of 'this harmony and order which pervades the
physical world'. The important matter is to acquiesce to the fact
of Professor Davies's assertion that 'the laws of the Universe,
from quarks to quasars, dovetail together so felicitously that
the impression that there is something behind it all seems
overwhelming.'

1. Muḥyīddīn Ibn 'Arabī.

Unfortunately, Professor Davies seems to stop in fear that he might discover 'behind the miracle of physics' a 'designer' which might look like the 'traditional creator'. It seems odd on two accounts that Professor Davies does not appreciate the discrepancies entailed, dove or not. One, that there could be, if physically pursued, a coming into being from nothing – big, small or medium bang or no bang at all. The other is the 'traditional creator' – it is explicit in the realms of intensive integration into the nature of existence that there can be only one Creator *cum* created, thereby reducing or magnifying, as the stand-point of view or the end of the telescope describes, a single existent.

A third danger in matters, which up to now were esoteric (simply because the generality of the literate public was, so to speak, in its whizz-kid adolescence) and which are now in their outward expression, is to overlook the fact that they will require a definition, and will define by reason, that if the premise is such that there is only one single unique existent or existence, the nature of that can only be comprehended if there is a re-integration of that oneness by the one seeking to know. Obviously this procedure would demand a premise or a platform which would go beyond a formalised religion, which is very akin to a medieval concept of a town with its keep and encircling walls to which one either belonged or was excluded from 'intrusion' to its embracing, exclusive form. It would need to break down the walls of dogma and creed, enlarging its periphery to allow – in short, to tolerate – all other forms of belief by the sheer fact that all belief must irrevertibly concern the same one and only existent or existence.

Here we have to appeal to another writing of Professor Paul Davies, 'God and the New Physics'[2] as reviewed by Adrian Berry under the title 'God and The Big Bang'[3], and to tolerate that one is bound to take exception to a portion of what is

2. *God and the New Physics* by Paul Davies. Pelican, London, 1984.
3. *Daily Telegraph*, 15th June 1986.

exposed in the article; viz., that 'if we maintain that he (God) exists outside space and time' he should wish to apply to the process of verification of this 'unknown region of nothingness', as he calls it, an 'astronomical evidence' which has to do with 'space, time and matter'. How, if something is either nothing or outside the boundaries of our conceptual space, time and matter, does he wish us to elucidate that nothing through these means? It would seem obvious that for that which is 'outside space and time' one would need parameters equally outside space and time, therefore beyond the scope of relative thought or expression. Hence, to try and delve into a nature which, by its position, is left outside relative conception with the use of physics, which at best gives a relative impression of how things work, seems, at this juncture, as desuate as the dogmatic insistence on religion.

It would be to the credit of Professor Davies if he would carry forward the process of his enlightenment, as glimpsed from his hesitant assertions to reach beyond the present day syllabus of physical terminology and practice, and allow space to the visible, although conspicuously tremulous, innate impulse of intuitive elaboration of reason pregnant in his exposition of his thought. It is the required birthright of today that it should be allowed to benefit from a new expression of both religion and physics in the formulation of a new vision – and this vision is Beshara.

Beshara is the good omen for the coming age, where the equally entrenched dogmatic insistence upon religion and a denial of religion and God come together with clenched fists. Neither is a vacillating and consequently self-excusing washing down of the fall-out the answer; nor is 'scientificating' an *ex-cathedra* pontification in the guise of solution anything other than debasing the issue. The answer and achievement would lie in the domains of such as Professor Davies. They could evolve a *processus* to go beyond the confines of the present day's inherited and closely-kept procedures to coincide with the proposition which would emerge from an expansion beyond a stigmatised and meticulously closed conformity to an eroded dogmatism. Otherwise one has to prognosticate that, were Jesus to come a second time, both scientists and the people of the robe would at last come together to deny him without waiting for a cock to crow.

COOKING

Notice to Cooks

Now know this – that cooking is an art. It is also an integral part of esoteric training because it is a twofold means of service: service to humanity and service to the food prepared. There is no higher state than that which a man can reach; all other forms of life in this world find their possibility of reaching a higher state through their conjunction with man. The only possibility for the sublimation of some minerals, vegetables and animals in a higher state of life is through cooking. That is why the sect which has aligned itself to the great saint Jalaluddin of Rum, the Mevlevi, refer to the esoteric education of the novices as cooking, and to achievement as taste. Those who use ingredients of food without consideration of providing the best possible means of an ingredient's expression are devaluing service, awareness and value of life. Therefore, cooking is not a mixture of ingredients but a harmonious composition of artistic value, nutrient and transcendent, giving the possibility of the best expression to the ingredients as well as to the composition in general. It should be undertaken only in an attitude of deep respect and consideration and full awareness of the bounty and clemency in the Divine order.

Note – that there is no expression of divine manifestation devoid of beauty. Beauty of taste (*dhawq*) is an absolutely necessary ingredient of the essential (in all senses) composition. Had it been in the Divine order of things that mankind should graze, there would have been no need for cooking at all, but such not being the case, it is erroneous to think that all value in vegetables is only in a raw or under-cooked ingestion. Therefore certain fruits and vegetables have to be cooked properly before they can be eaten. The human being has neither tripe nor crop. Hence it is an incalculable error to think mankind could or should imitate avian or bestial mores.

Know then, that cooking is a responsibility in awareness wherein under-cooking or over-cooking are equally reprehensible and a clear oversight.

May the *himma* of the great saint who was Rumi's personal cook till his death, Şemseddin Ateşbaz Walī, be upon you who undertake to serve in this kitchen.

Introduction to Turkish Cookery

The French, who pride themselves on their fine cooking, which, to say the least, they have evolved into an art, admit to the existence of three main 'cuisines' in the world. Naturally, they think the first is French, and the other two are the Chinese and the Byzantine-Ottoman.

History

The variety and richness of this cookery is a direct result of the fascinating history of these lands. There is no room here to go into the geographical and physical origins milleniums back. But later in the history of the Roman Empire, one can trace the major trends that led to the making of the Eastern Mediterranean cookery. The Byzantine Empire, which succeeded the Roman, used to be known as the Eastern Roman Empire, with its capital in Constantinople, a town so named because of its founder, the Roman Emperor Constantine. It ruled all the eastern territories, mingling all the cultures of the Eastern Mediterranean and those of the lands beyond its Eastern boundaries, as far as Armenia, Persia and beyond. Roman cookery had been at best crude in comparison, until Rome became an Empire. The turning point came when Julius Caesar first took over Ptolemaic Egypt with its capital in Alexandria.

Alexandria had already evolved its cookery and was renowned for its banquets, which most often ended in orgies. This the Roman Empire took over. Later, with this heritage was mixed the Eastern influences coming from Persia and the Middle East in general.

The Turks, who called themselves Ottoman after their first leader, came upon this scene a little later, bringing with them tastes and influences which stretch back to Samarkand, Balkh or Bukhara.

General Rules for Planning a Turkish Meal

In the French 'cuisine', the menu is the prime co-ordinator of what should be eaten at a meal, which is considered a unit. The Chinese meal is a composite mosaic of tastes. The Eastern Mediterranean meal is a co-ordinated variety, linked together with the relationship of each of the component parts. Here tastes do not follow each other in sequence, as in a menu.

An Eastern Mediterranean menu does not exist as such. Often some dishes, as in the Chinese way, are served together, so that those who wish can eat them at the same time, mixing them up in their own plates.

Variety

The Turkish meal offers a variety of tastes linked together, each part a distinct taste served during the same meal because they 'go together'. One must taste a little of this and a little of that. No imposed general context must run through the meal. The art of preparing a menu for a meal in true Eastern Mediterranean cookery depends on one's fore-knowledge of what 'goes together'.

Choice

There must be an alternative to each dish contained in the menu, in case someone would prefer something else. It is rude to dislike food, but a possibility of choice must always be given. One would think that this is a rule which may not be often observed easily nowadays, with modern prices. But portions are usually small. The food placed before the people partaking of the meal is varied, thereby compensating amply for the lack of bigger portions. It is considered rather rude, at least indelicate, to serve heaps of food. Guests have been known to murmur in disgust once the back of the host is turned: '... as if we had just come out of acute misery.' On the other hand, to give exact portions, like, say, four baked potatoes for four people, is considered even worse and unforgivable. Beside seeming miserly, it allows guests to think that what they are offered is counted – inadmissible within the rules of hospitality.

Balance

One rule for everyone to remember, is never serve one 'heavy' dish with another. It must be followed by a 'light' one.

Another rule, is never to serve acids with other acids. It is a custom always to serve lemon with every fish dish. Therefore it would be considered barbarian to serve yoghurt in the same meal. In fact, fish and yoghurt must never appear together in the same dish or menu. There are some who insist that the combination might easily end in death as an acute indigestion is certain. When pastry dishes are served, yoghurt appears again always to tone down the 'heaviness' of pastry and rice. But rice is served in every meal, as Pilaff always, and as the last course before sweets, unless someone has directly asked for it to be served with some vegetable or meat, or the famous dried beans which in Turkey is often eaten mixed with the pilaff.

In short, it is all a matter of 'finesse'. One has to experience judgement and discretion. Consequently a Turkish meal is a composite of different individual tastes, combined – but not blended – and woven into one pattern.

Taste

This idea of composition is also the underlying theory in Turkish cookery. Each dish is not necessarily a complex taste, produced by the many ingredients that go into its making. On the contrary, the taste of the original item, from which the dish most often draws its name, must be prominently present; the rest of the ingredients only enhance the special taste of the main ingredient. A composition, so to speak, where the leit-motif is ever present in all its variations.

The amalgamate taste was then exercised for centuries, worked and refined to form this cookery. The centre of this was, and is still, Istanbul – or Constantinople as it used to be known in the old days. The Ottoman Empire, which continued the Byzantine and extended from Vienna to Fez in Morocco, naturally left its culinary imprint on all the countries under its rule for several centuries, in varying degrees. Turkey, which forms the compact nucleus of this influence, is the theme of this book. Several hundred years of rule with a centralised capital as an arbiter of taste and customs has naturally more or less unified this cookery, allowing only a few regional variants.

Foods

Of all food, vegetables in Turkish cookery have an honoured place to themselves as in no other cookery. They form dishes in their own right, not as mere side dishes or 'garniture' for meat, etc., but as definite courses in the context of the meal. They are exceptional in taste and variety, where each vegetable flavour is flattered to assert itself under its own name and taste. This is partly due to the fact that Istanbul boasts of three things unequalled elsewhere, and one of these is vegetables. The other two are the fish and the water. The result is that the fish dishes have taken on an importance, and have given rise to some exceptional treatment. Waters of Istanbul used to be prized

70

like vintage wine in the old days, each source or spring being qualified with special merits and taste.

Cooking Methods

An onion base is important in almost all dishes. This might well have been the origin of the French *soubise*, which, with the *mirepoix*, forms one of the two main sauce foundations prepared externally in the French culinary art. Nearly all vegetables are what in cookery terms is known as *mijoté* – cooked very slowly and well covered. To achieve the best results, it is perhaps most convenient to bring the food to a quick boil, with intense heat. Then reduce the heat at once and well cover the pot, and leave it to cook until very tender and until the juices are reduced. Usually, small cooking-pots are preferred. A plate, upside down, is placed directly over the vegetables, fitting loosely into the cooking pot, before the lid is placed on. This plate is never touched, even when the lid is removed to inspect the progress of the cooking. The plate is lifted out only when the dish is ready and the vegetables are to be turned out.

The next step is to drain away the juice and to keep it warm. Then, the serving plate which will carry the vegetables to the table is placed upside down over the cooking pot. Holding the two together, the whole thing is turned over. When the cooking pot is removed, one can see that the vegetables have remained in exactly the same layered position as originally arranged. Then, one should add the still-warm juice and serve.

Vessels

The cooking vessels most often used for these vegetables are round-bottomed like an inverted dome. They are made of beaten copper and lined inside and out with lead. This method of cooking was considered the most delicate. It is known as *kuşhane* which means 'bird's home', another way of saying

71

nest-shaped. For larger dishes which will not be turned over but will be served in the pot where they have been cooked, an earthenware dish is chosen. For the *Türlü* which we shall see later, this is essential as it is finished in the oven and served very hot.

Sauces

External sauces which tend to unify the taste of all ingredients are disliked, except for boiled food where a sauce, separately prepared, is allowed to be added on.

Juices, however, are absolutely essential. They must be naturally reduced without any thickening matter being added. If the dish is 'dry', it is the sign of a negligent cook. On the other hand, if the juices are too abundant or liquid, then the famous Turkish phrase which denotes tastelessness is mercilessly applied – sometimes to describe even a human being – 'itself to one side, its juices to another', to mean a complete lack of cohesion.

Flavouring

Moderation is the golden rule of everything. This applies absolutely to food. All excess is frowned upon by good taste. Such things as garlic, which is now being used in the West with the zeal of the neophyte, should therefore be used with great care and very sparingly. Garlic can easily smother all other tastes and aromas which should be present and detectable.

Only certain foods require mixed spicing. Usually a single spice or herb is used in any one dish, except for parsley which may accompany another.

Special Regional Characteristics

In the South Eastern parts, adjacent to Arab territories of the old Empire, hot food is emphasised. In the region of Konya, the ancient Iconium which later became the capital of the Seljuk Turks before the arrival of the Ottomans, fat was lavishly used. In general, provincial food in this section of the world is reduced to a few dishes in each place. The majority is a uniform cookery valid for the whole of Turkey, with the best prototypes still to be found in Istanbul, the city which remained an Imperial capital over one thousand and one hundred years, the longest in all the history of the world. This is the undoubted centre of this cuisine.

Istanbul

The centre of Ottoman and/or Turkish cookery, Istanbul has imposed a rule and a taste on all dishes. They must be 'light'. The best expression, therefore, of all cooking in Turkey is embodied in these prototypes of Istanbul cooking. Only a few dishes are allowed in from the regions beyond Istanbul. The rest of the regional arrangements in cookery are considered *kaba* – unrefined – therefore 'heavy'. Istanbul is fastidious.

Vegetables are always most delectable when they are yet tender and in their early season. This is known as being *turfanda*, therefore, also more expensive. Istanbul came to accept the idea of imported vegetables from other parts of Turkey, outside their season in Istanbul, with great diffidence and very reluctantly. Where it was a custom to stuff the flower of the courgette because the vegetable itself was yet too small – not more than half an inch – so as to serve it *turfanda*, this is understandable.

Consequent to the reforms in Turkey, when everything had to be sold by the kilo according to the metric system, the murmur of discontent was thunderous in protest as a distant storm. *Bamya* – ladies' fingers or ochra – used to be sold by the dozen.

73

They had to be very small, not longer than an inch. The new system of selling by weight brought forth the bigger, coarser *bamya* to the market.

Each vegetable was considered best if it came from fields in a particular section of the sprawling town, spread over two continents at once.

The above-mentioned *bamya* should come from Maltepe; the aubergines from Bekār Deresi near Çengelköy on the Bosphorus; the artichokes from Bayram Paşa, or better still, from Sarayiçi, a small field of artichokes within the walls of the Topkapi Palace. The amateurs would wait early after dawn by the gates to buy off the all-too-few artichokes that came out of the back garden gate of the Topkapi Palace.

Unexplained habits and saying attached to vegetables used to be repeated as undoubted truths. The courgettes were known as 'Paradise Food', the aubergines were considered as the 'Prophet's elect' – perhaps he had met with them in Damascus, who knows? One should never eat leeks after March. Whoever eats broad-beans for forty days will surely lose all their mental capacities and turn imbecile. Besides, after early spring this vegetable was too coarse, no one would eat it. One did not drink water while eating *bamya*; it would be considered barbarous. When Sultan Reshad received Enver Paşa at lunch because the Paşa had married a princess, the Sultan seemed quite favourably inclined to the Paşa according to what he told of his meeting, until he said (or so it is told) once in the privacy of his own quarters, that he was astounded to see the Paşa drink a sip of water after eating *Bamya*!

On the other hand, it is customary to take a sip of water after eating artichokes (– it is true that this turns into a very pleasant sweet taste in the mouth), but not after figs from Karak on the Black Sea entrance to the Bosphorus. From Erenköy come the Çavuş grapes, walnuts from Beykoz, and the extraordinarily fragrant pink strawberries from Emirgan, all the other fruit ranges over outlying districts. The Black Sea port of Giresun, the ancient Cerisonte, was the home of cherries, from whence Lucullus, the Roman general, the most famous of the gourmets of the old world, introduced them into Rome in the early years AD; but now they come from Bursa. The water-melon comes from Tekirdağ on the European shores, but melons must be from Manisa in Asia Minor. Apples from Amasya, but pears from Ankara, white peaches from Edirne but yellow ones from Bursa. Chestnuts from a small locality called Inkaya on the slopes of the Prussian Olympus, and the hazel-nuts from Karamürsel on the gulf of Nicodemia on the Black Sea.

The fish, except for the red mullet which must be caught in Pendik, must all come from the Bosphorus. No other fish is considered nearly as tasty, and among them, the most esteemed of them all are the *lüfer*, which must be caught in the full moons of the autumn months. Most of this is not a matter of fancy devoid of truth. The fish go up the Bosphorus to the Black Sea, which is much less salty than the Mediterranean, to spawn. When they are just about mature, the young tender fish come down the Bosphorus on their way to the Mediterranean. Then they are caught and are truly exceptional in taste. The mackerel, in February when a few of them make up a kilo, are the right size for making that delicious dish, *Uskumru Dolması* – Stuffed Mackerel – to be eaten cold the next day. But between the *lüfer* season and the smaller summer fish, is the time when the un-equalled *kalkan* (turbot) reigns supreme, defying any comparison with its North Sea cousin.

After spoiling one's taste in Istanbul, it is rare to wish to repeat it elsewhere, and certainly impossible to match it. But we shall now see how some these extravaganzas of the culinary art are prepared. I shall give only the basic recipes. Each would-be chef can vary these according to his or her own temperament and mood for adventure and artistic expression.

A well-known restaurant of great renown in Istanbul is Abdullah Efendi. This is the nearest to the best Istanbul home cooking – an art which was fast dying until some time ago. In the old days, when wealthy and large houses still existed, the cooks used to come invariably from one section of Anatolia: Bolu. I hear there is now a good place in Bolu on the auto-route to Ankara where the Istanbul tradition is kept up.

There are many small-scale restaurants on the upper Bosphorus where fish can be had. In town, Pandelli's over the entrance to the Spice Bazaar was also famous for its fish dishes.

In Sirkeci is the Konya Restaurant which, in spite of its name, has adopted Istanbul cookery; it is an excellent place to eat, though more primitive.

Döner kebab is a kebab that is on a vertical spit. The best place anywhere to eat this was at a small, very primitive place in Parmakkapi. It was cooked under the eyes of the passers-by and was succulent. However, perhaps some ideas of hygiene or perhaps a misconception of aesthetics has now obliterated this visual as well as olfactory indulgence.

WRITINGS

The Child Across Time

I have never felt the compulsion to write all that has happened to me through life. I had to be told I must. Now at the peak of 75 years, looking back, I can see almost photographically and with sentiment all the memories of times past in review in the eye of my mind, some happy and some pleasant, some sad and bad, and nearly all glad to be relegated to my past-present, which enables me to think that some of them have been instrumental, most assuredly, in forming my present-future. I look forward, then, to a future which I already taste and savour as an alluring possibility in store, awaiting its time, the whistle or the gun which will start it on its, God knows, how many metres dash across time.

Nothing has been slow; leisurely often but even then fast, the right length of time-span to scent the lovely taste of its duration, grateful when over, as it removes its own iron-hold and sensitive strain of extreme pleasure or the deserved quantity of its merit with its pain.

In a way, I am Swinburnian. Pleasure seems to be often the alluring, enticing, leaven of pain. But again, with him, I find that, not one's entire life, but the lives of one's life-long episodes of life 'endure' only 'for a span' – and again I carry my concordance with him to the belief in the 'Holy Spirit of Man', as solace and an aim within reach before death do us part this world and we enter life eternal. The Perfectibility of Man seems that promise in which hope and comfort, not only psychological but as a true practical possibility, draws one on, helping one round the asperities of life and living till that day when, like that 'weariest river', one 'winds somewhere safe to sea'.

One's life seems to follow an anthological pattern of varied vibrations corresponding not to one central *leit-motif* but to many chords and dischords, finalising into a harmony which is one's own theme and, at the end, to one's own particular 'swan-song'.

I have always wanted to end, not in slow expiation and demise like an echo fading after a repetitious resounding into no consequential response, but rather to come to a deliberate stop, not induced but culminatingly decisive, and then to expire with a true and willing giving up of a relative state depending on the availability of oxygen, with a not-too-sustained aspirant, elegant and eloquent in its deliberate exhalation, like a romantic adieu softly but audibly tracing its sound into a slightly drawn *Hū*.

If I had thought that all my life had been spent in a faded sepia picture-book quietude, I would have rebelled for life, and a constant, imperative, compulsive ebb and tide of blood in the arteries of my past days. Fortune smiled – I had a sonorous, crescending tympanum beating in the temples of Beethovian resonance. Miltonian eloquence and the temper of the *Paradise Lost* gave constant revival, in strength of expression alone to my humour of those days when I prospered among the Pyramids of Egypt, where sand at my feet, fertilised, gave fruit to vie with the best of the prolific world.

However, all these were moods. They passed and were placed with contrasting patchworks of the many coats of Joseph, in colour and variety of material and texture. I am like the moon, the major water sign, Cancer. Cancer is supposed to be variable, indirect like a crab, ruled by an ever changing moon racing from crescent to full and back again.

It is not true; the constancy of the moon is misunderstood. The face the moon shows is always the same, reacting to moods as required. But the secret face of the moon, its unseen face, is as secret, constant and enduring as the hermetic mystery of a tri-majestic divinity.

So it was, and it is Cancer that rules through my horoscope. Now the Aquarian age – and by that regressive count the origin of the present emergence of man – falls at once after Cancer. Two thousand years of Pisces that has introduced the advent of Aquarius was preceded by two thousand years of the Egyptian Aries of Ptah, to whose preponderant divinity is dedicated the impressive grand avenue of rams at Karnak. Prior to that era was the rule of the Sacred Bull of the lower Egypt, where the carefully carved tombs of the divine emblems of the cycle run endless avenues below the sands of Sakkarah. Before them is the Gemini: the twins, boy and girl mark the couple, parent progenitors on earth, biblically banished from Heaven 'they two hand in hand took their solitary way, the world was before them where they choose ...' and begin the life of this emergence of man. But life on Earth comes from water – the Cancer, the moon to whose attraction water is still bound, enslaved in a flow of ebb and tide for ever.

Born on the 17th of July in 1911 by water's edge on the Asian shores of the Bosphorus in Beylerbeyi, Istanbul, I was endowed with the riches of the Ottoman Empire's sway against the background of the Byzantine opulence of ancient Constantinople. This was a town built no more like the 'blind' Calcedonians nor the astute colonisers of Byzas built; not on one shore or cove or haven, but on the converging shores of two continents where, instead of a river like the Seine in Paris or even the Thames in London, the sea undertook to flow an ever wondrous current, between the two continents, Asia and Europe, dividing East from West – and what is more significant, it unified them into one perpetual metropolis for which the sea forms a thoroughfare and assumes an isthmuseity, to separate but hold together equally a world of possibilities, counter balanced by facts of what has unavoidably to be by the exigencies of its own nature. This town where I was born has now been chosen for a human dream of Peace as the Capital of a United World.

* * *

81

The story of my childhood naturally starts in this two world ambience in the well-to-do circumstances of an immense park, ranging from the hill-tops down to the sea. Our nanny, Miss Nichols, dominates the hazy scene of childhood memories of pleasure – and perhaps pain, but the mind sifts, in its beneficence, that which is pleasant to hold, and that which is unpleasant is cast out never to be remembered again. It may be that I was a lucky child endowed with such a munificent gift of retaining only pleasure. I am indeed grateful for this, although I remain an unfashionable person by the requirements of today, where, to be somebody, you have to have had a childhood both of physical and mental want and agony. Be that as it may, if I am to brand myself not-common for those circumstances of pleasure, I am prone to agree that not only in that domain but in many others I was indeed an un-common child, growing inexorably, taking in all that goes to make one exceptional – and blessing God for it – I was indeed endowed with all the worldly affluence possible, and with an excellent parental environment of affection wherein I, the second son of the two children that my parents had, flourished with a peculiar growing memory which has stood the test of years and accompanied me to here.

Moods do change, Cancer or not, and one is constantly in a different configuration at every instant. And movement is life. It is hard to imagine life as a static, immobile existence. Even the sloth moves through and along the bough – upside down and slow, but it moves and is alive. There is no energy which does not 'move' in some way or sense even when it is static. So slowly, often so slow that it was akin to laziness, with which I was often accused, I grew to acquire a ponderous reaction to the surrounding circumstances, a grave, calculating attitude hiding a bent for humour, laughter and pleasure.

It was before the end of my third year that Miss Nichols had to leave so as not to be incarcerated in some interior part of the country so many regulation miles away from the sea. The British were enemies, so were the French, many secondary

82

states and Russia. But Russia did not so much count, as Russians were age-old enemies anyhow and their animosity had even entered age-old adages. What it all meant was that what I knew of nursery rhymes – there was a goodly bunch of them – was all that I would know. From then on, one did not aspire to learn or speak English. However, from that which remained in memory I used to translate to my maternal grandmother, whose favourite grandson I was, while she lay in search of sleep on her night-sofa where she passed the night. This was in her dressing room where she passed most of the day. Two large sofas faced each other, while arm-chairs stood around and large comfortable cushions lay on the floor.

Everything happened in this rather large room except meals. One of the rooms that opened out from her boudoir was her private drawing room where she rarely sat except when there was a real guest to receive, not an important guest but a guest all the same, and when she had her meals a small table was laid fully garnished with silver and plates. There she had her meals with one or two people: me, of course, when I was visiting grandmother, just the two of us sometimes by the low extending windows of the *yalı* (house by the water) overlooking the constant flow of the Bosphorus.

After lunch she retired to her siesta, and I never knew which of her sofas she slept in of an afternoon because I would be taken to my room to be told to sleep and to make no noise because grandmother would be sleeping. Not that I could have awakened her even if I had all the noise in my power to pour out. We lived in separate quarters of the immense building which housed grandmother's two hundred ladies that looked after her and her house. But so it was. I was silenced because I had been told grandmother would sleep in her boudoir.

Her bedroom was a monumental affair containing a massive four-poster bed with curtains and pelmets gathered up into a crown from whence descended again drapes at the back of the two sides of the bed. I never saw them down. Always gathered with thick cords and huge golden tassels opening to light the enormous, high bed, which required two deep coral red velvet covered steps to take one up to bed. I was not really allowed in that room, but once in a while I could escape unseen and try the extraordinary circumstance of going to bed on velvet steps. To keep it without noise, quiet and calm, this room was not on the sea front but at the back, and its windows opened to grandmother's park, which was far larger than anything we had. Somewhere up on the hillside below false rockery and birds, it also had a lake with an island in it for the musicians.

Grandmother had inherited this *yalı* and its *Koru* (a wooded park) from her mother and two other ladies who were equally wives of her father, my great-grandfather on my mother's side. This ancestor was the well known Khedive of Egypt, Ismail, the one who opened the Suez Canal with so much pomp and circumstance that to entertain his guests during their stay in Egypt he had, among other things, the Cairo Opera House built. He had commissioned Guiseppe Verdi to write *Aida*, with its ancient Egyptian tragic love affair, gleaned from the hieroglyphics on the walls of tombs, for the first performance and Grand Overture. Partly due to Verdi's phobia of sea-travel, the plan back-fired. *Aida* was not ready for its world premiere in Cairo, but the Cairo Opera House did all the same entertain the Royal guests with other operas. My introduction to operatic music and performance was with *Aida* and in Cairo when I was nine years old. The stage still used the original sets, and the glittering *Ritorna Vincitor* of Radames, standing on a palanquin in the full glory of the conqueror, slowly carried on the shoulders of Nubians towards the front of the stage, shone dazzling, impressive with the accompaniment of the full strength of the chorus. Indelibly, it left in me a taste for opera and added to a wonderment that had been building up in me ever since that very first December morning, when I woke up and saw the brilliant sunshine of Egypt with the white-stalked Imperial palms shining in the light and the bougainvillea spreading an irrepressible pattern of purple over the scene. Ever since, I thought Egypt was a worldly paradise – and it could have been had it not condescended to the state of a 'developing African nation' only politically and economically concerned, forgetting its soul and spirit, which, if revived and cared for, would have made of that land known as the 'Gift of the Nile' a treasury of well being not only for itself but for many a part of the world.

The second opera I saw was dramatic in another way. A childish envy and desire, never to be satisfied, arose in me, branding me with a love of lakes and ducks and geese and all aquatic birds, from giant white egrets to swans alike. To see on stage, there before one's eyes, a knight, helm and sword and all, ride on a magnificent white swan across the lake and disappear from sight and sound was too alluring – and it was something one could never achieve, except in dreams perhaps, and that was another world of reality with which I had already a contact when I was three; a dream which remained indelibly with me, even to this day, in all its glorious colour and significance. Today I look upon that dream as a corroborative consequence of a dream my mother had when she was heavily pregnant with me. She saw a name written in a light which reminded her of lights used in those days for celebration illuminations, and wondered what festivity was being celebrated. She was told in her dream that the light she saw written in the sky over the hills on the opposite side of the Bosphorus was the name of the son she was bearing in her womb. So I was named before I was born, so sure she was of the veracity of her dream. I certainly was not born nor grew as a dream-child, but in time I grew more convinced that, in general, people live in a dream, only to wake up once their bodies are laid down to an eternal rest and sleep. All the same, life on earth is a gift and a blessing. Very few nowadays are privileged to inhale the staggering smell of wet earth after the rain, almost sensuous, an enveloping satisfaction, harmonising, essentially, with the being and make-up of man. Such things in life dictate the unavoidable unity of all that is; not as all making up the one, but that the essence which is one is all that there is on earth, in the universes, and in all that there is as eleven dimensions and eternity. Blake's 'grain of sand' in the 'palm of one's hand' takes on a reality which, in spite of the strangeness of his drawings, is certainly most satisfying and promising as a vision of Truth.

When I first saw Egypt, she was a bustling land where all of Europe met during winter sleet and cold. From everywhere people flocked, not only to soak up the perpetual sunshine and enjoy the roses of winter (which are at their best in January), but also to steep themselves in an impelling presence of man's past. Egypt, for the Mediterranean basin, is a consciousness of man's civilisation. To limit man's or Europe's ancestry to a classicist predilection for Greece is blinding man's historic evolutionary progress by blinkering its vision to a narrow lane of latter-day heritage without antecedent and procedure. A European culture without Mosaic inheritance is nothing other than an easy- lazy thought and the delusion born of a negative, misunderstood Christianity which chose to establish its church by coercion and inquisitory compulsion, like the later resurgence of the same practices in the shape of the Gestapo or the KGB, down to today's loathsome apartheid. African man was probably an original forebear, as Leakey would have it. Once we admit Ancient Egypt into the rich pattern of our ancestral cultural lineage, we are bound to find that many of our self-imposed falsehoods will be falling off and that our social toil within the trials of man's emancipation becomes automatically easier.

I come from a pure Caucasian stock with some Albanian and a good chunk of Turkish thrown in. On my mother's side, my great-grandmother was Georgian, my great-grandfather was of a mixture of Turkish, Circassian and probably Albanian descent. Their second daughter was my grandmother, who I remember as living only in Emirgan on the European shore of the upper Bosphorus. Her garden, what is left of it beyond the building line near the shore, is now a municipal park. The kiosk in it, once burnt down, is now repaired as a quasi-Swiss Chalet and is run by the Automobile Club with a restaurant for small snacks. I remember that pavilion very well before it was burnt down. The ceiling of the main floor was painted blue with golden stars everywhere in it. Because the Sultan Abdül Aziz, who was a friend to Ismail Pasha, my great-grandfather, wanted to come and visit him, Ismail I – the Khedive (Viceroy) of Egypt – had that pavilion built in fifteen days with people working day and night with lamps.

The Sultan came on horseback and Ismail Pasha, who was waiting for him at the upper gate of the *Koru*, led the Sultan on horseback down to this pavilion by the bridle of the horse. All this was hospitality, very true, but high-pitched as a deft but excessive, theatrical *mise-en-scène*. The abode of the Khedive was supposedly to be deemed too humble to receive the Ottoman Sultan, the Caliph of all the Moslems, whose titles and styles included the 'ruler of the four corners of the world' and 'of the Seven Seas', and as if that was not enough and also to add a touch of supreme holiness, 'the Shadow of God on Earth'!

The reality, however, was not only that. The Khedive wanted something from the Sultan and was willing to pay for it, and the Sultan wanted the pay, which he needed badly. The other desire of the Sultan had already been thwarted by the viziers of the Sultan and had already been relegated to oblivion. No, the fact that the Sultan had unwisely fallen under the charm of the eldest daughter of the Khedive of Egypt, the Princess Tawhida, was by now a past episode. While it had lasted, the Sultan had assigned the Beylerbeyi Palace to the wife and the two daughters of the Khedive, where they stayed for fifteen days as the guest of the Sultan. These had been fifteen difficult days for the government of the Empire.

The princess in question was attractive beyond doubt with her reddish hair, wonderful complexion, and short-sighted blue eyes which she used with great coquetterie and *savoir-faire*. But since the time of Osman II, who was deposed and brutally murdered, no Sultan was allowed to marry into the family of a notable of the Empire. To marry the Khedive's daughter would have given the rich Khedive of Egypt an unbalanced preponderance over everyone else in the realm. The rowing boat of the grand vizier crossed the Bosphorus eleven times one day, but the Sultan relented. Messengers were sent out to all the Circassian villages of Anatolia to bring back an exact replica of the Princess of Egypt. It was done. The Sultan was satisfied. The presents he sent to the two daughters were priceless. A butterfly made of five huge diamonds about four inches in length and breadth for the elder daughter, and a diamond brooch for grandmother which later, sold by her, paid for the building of the Ministry of Agriculture in Cairo and the building and the partial endowment of the Faculty of Literature of the University of Cairo – the rest of the endowment coming from other sources of riches of the richest woman of Egypt while she lived.

But her eldest sister had been richer than her. However, the Princess Tawhida loved to dress up in clothes for which the material had to be bought at the factory so that no one else could make a dress from the same material. Her store rooms were full of rolls upon rolls of cloth out of which had been taken only one length for a dress. Taking such tastes and inclinations into consideration, it would be not at all difficult to conclude that the Princess would fall into debt at times. But she had a solution for that too. She used to diet for a fortnight and keep herself completely in darkened rooms. At the end of that time she used to emerge really drawn and wan. Putting on a very simple black velvet gown to enhance her pallor, girded by an emblematic iron chain dangling to the floor from her waist, she used to visit her father the Khedive. The picture had its desired effect, and the solicitous parent would query after the health of his daughter. Her answer was that, no, she was not physically

88

ill except that she suffered from being the **slave** of her creditors. That was the chosen word known to have effect on the proud potentate father. 'No daughter of mine can be a slave – let her creditors be paid!' Yet, when it came to pass that the father, the Khedive Ismail of Egypt, was removed from office by the Sultan on the insistence of the creditor powers of Europe for debts that Egypt could not pay soon enough, even the Finance Minister of the Khedive, the mighty Armenian, Ubor Pasha, threw up his hands in despair, and the Khedive left his post and rule and went into exile. The Princess could not face the situation even though she had a great deal of income still at her command. In her sorrow, she had the shutters closed and took morphine for fifteen days and died. A very sad story.

Fortunately her younger sister, the Princess Fatima, the grandmother we talk about, was not of the same bent. Equally uneconomic, but married to a very sick Prince whom she survived. When her husband died in his early twenties, he left her with two children with a palace at Benha and other lands under cultivation, bringing in a great deal of income. All the same, to live like she did the expenditure was enormous. The young widow soon found a romantic affair which ended in her second marriage. The second husband was a Circassian come over from the Caucasus to study at the Islamic University of Al-Azhar. His relative, a Circassian clan relationship, was the wife of the Egyptian Pasha who looked after the affairs of the young widow. There was a state portrait of the princess in the drawing room of the Pasha's wife. When the young Circassian saw the portrait, he said that was the lady he would marry! His 'aunt' laughed at the audacious idea; the Khedive's daughter to marry the student, a pauper and stateless since the Russian persecution!

One night at the palace of the Princess, a fire broke out. All rushed around, including the young Circassian who was staying with his 'aunt'. The fire had caught some of the curtains, which could be seen from the staircase where the Princess was watching the scene from behind the screen of the banisters. People could not easily approach the curtains because they were really ablaze. The Circassian walked up to them, dauntless, tore them down with his hands and stamped on them to put them out. The Princess watched, fell in love, and married him without another thought! He tripled her income and that is how she became the richest woman in Egypt. After his death, grandmother lived on in Emirgan with her retinue of women, eunuchs and serving maids, going to Egypt during the winters, taking over the whole ship, there and back to Istanbul, until the First World War years came. She died some years after the World War ended. I remember her on board when I went with father to say good-bye and wish her a good journey; and that was her last trip to Egypt and the last time she took over the boat and the Captain's quarters. The boat was still painted in battleship grey and was named Ex-Aurora from Ottawa. She used to send the carpenters on board a long time before sailing date and have the Captain's quarters altered to her requirements, and a bed, just like a sofa, large and low, was fitted in. From the Captain down, all the crew received a double monthly pay for the trip and suitable presents, like the most valuable cuff-links for the Captain and lesser gold or silver useful jewellery for the others.

She took with her a whole lot of people, families and friends, to pass the winter with her. Some came back with her and some earlier, but always at her expense. She was generous in a strange way. If she had her way with people she was very generous, or if the person was unknown to her but needed help, through the intervention of someone she trusted she would provide continuous help to every detail of their need. For herself, she needed show. Being small she wore very high heels. She would receive people she wanted to impress standing at the top of the stairs with a turban and a high curving feather held by a jewel, so that when people looked up they saw this imposing figure waiting for their ascent to where she stood. If she could not put on a show, she preferred not to perform. For instance, when she went to the palace, her accompanying lady would always be decked with some very valuable jewellery in an eye-catching setting, lent her for the occasion, while she herself would wear a large single stone somewhere on her body.

In her later years she was restricted materially because of the war, she being in Turkey and her source of income in Egypt, now under enemy rule. Now in old age and beginning to ail, doctors advised her to go to Karlsbad which was thought to be a health-giving spa; but she would complain that she could not afford it. She explained why she could not afford it in this way: she would need to take the whole floor of the best hotel, have six black eunuchs with her retinue of ladies. All six eunuchs would be dressed in dark blue with what is known as a Brandenburg buttoning across the chest, the fastenings ending in silver tassels strung with coral beads. That would be six such tassels on each one of the six eunuchs at least. One would sit on each carriage next to the coachmen, who would have to wear her livery. When she went to take the waters, the pavilion would be closed to all except her party of six carriages, each carriage leaving the hotel with two ladies and going to the watering pavilion and returning to the hotel where the rest of her retinue of ladies would be waiting to receive her. Even her food would be partially prepared by her own cook, brought with her, while the rest of her retinue may eat the hotel food. Naturally she never went!

At seventy-odd, she returned to her beloved Egypt for the last time. When she first touched the Egyptian soil she went down on her hands and knees and kissed the earth, heedless of the people gathered to welcome her. Or was it totally heedless? She really loved Egypt, and she used to pray that she did not die until she returned there after the war; and so it happened. Her will was in keeping with her style. Her fortune was to be divided into four. One fourth was for the University of Cairo, one fourth was for the military and naval schools at the seat of the caliphate, wherever that may be. One fourth was for the people who had been in her service and to all their progeny and descendants for ever, and only the last fourth for the four children she left behind, a fourth of her palace to each with enough money entailed to be paid out to the servants as monthly salaries, and of course a large number of *feddans* (a kind of Egyptian acreage) for her four heirs and their children for all the generations to follow. My mother was the only daughter among the four heirs and she was allowed to choose pieces of artistic value. I remember a pendant, the head of a black Nubian with shiny brilliant eyes and with a white turban made of one white huge baroque pearl. More valuable than that was a carved emerald head of Leopold of Belgium in his childhood, looking like a cherub, with diamond studded wings. This was a brooch, and from between the wings which held the cherubic emerald head hung down a lovely drop-shaped emerald. There was another emerald, I remember, but this was not set like a piece of jewellery to wear. It was the head of the Empress Maria Theresa of Austria, crown and all, carved from one piece of flawless emerald. As mother did not often wear jewellery, her collection remained locked in two medieval-looking walnut trunks with high round tops and gilt metal bars running down over and across the trunks where they locked.

Grandmother's poverty was very relative. In the *yalı* at Emirgan where she lived, there were upstairs and downstairs halls long and large enough to run a horse race, from one end of which, upstairs, there extended corridors to her proper dining room, her several drawing rooms and to her conservatory with large pond and all. From the other side, one entered her rooms and the living quarters of her retinue of ladies. Downstairs were rooms for male attendants, eunuchs, secretaries, etc.

The house we lived in had also been hers. It actually had fifteen rooms, but it was the *Selāmlik* of the main house which was higher up on the hillside looking down on the winding wonder of the Bosphorus. The main house was the *Harem* where grandmother had been living and where mother had been born.

This *Selāmlik* (which means a reception house for male guests) was lower down the hillside. It was more manageable, and what was more important, it was nearer to the kitchens. It sounds odd. However, the kitchens in these old big houses were never in the same building. Always at some distance from the main house, food was brought into the living quarters in four-and-a-half-foot wooden trays covered with oil-cloth and a convex cupola-like cover with a brass knob on top. This dome-like lid to the tray was made of some light trellis material covered over in red camel skin. It kept the food warm through its journey from the kitchens to the houses, summer or winter. There were special carriers for these food trays which were called *tabla* and the carriers *tablacilars*. They were usually from a region called Shebin Karahisar, tall and erect, and with strong backs and necks, presumably. They carried the *tabla* on their heads. They wore a soft fez, a normal head gear, which they flattened to hold a two-inch-wide circle of tightly wound cloth to make a ring about six inches in diameter. This they placed over the fez, and on this ring was placed, very carefully centralised, the laden *tabla* with the whole long menu of those days from soup to pudding with the unavoidable pilaff, several vegetables, meats and böreks – and not a drop fell on the *tabla* from the kitchen to the house, through rain or shine, hot summer days or frozen winters. It is recorded that only once the *tablaci* Ali Dede slipped. Otherwise this *tablacilar*, who retired as a venerated Sheikh, much esteemed and visited by many, had carried the *tabla* from the kitchens to the *Harem* up on the hill without a hitch for many years, more than a mile, twice a day and sometimes three. During Ramadan, the month of Islamic Fast, before sunset (as one broke the fast at sunset), himself fasting, and sometimes in the night (as one finished eating sometime before dawn), he used to start his *zikr* (a rememoration of God through repetition of His Name) once the huge circular tray was balanced on his head, turning his head from to side at each enunciation of the Name, and the red leather covered dome

93

describing quarter circles, now to the right, now to the left. All the while the man advanced in measured steps along the tree lined avenue, fir trees on the ravine side and lilacs on the other.

The big house, the *Harem* where the ladies lived and received female and male guests, was half way up the steep slope to the mountain top. Male guests, not relatives, husbands not accompanying their wives, were not entertained there. There were men living in the *Harem* but either they were intimates or relatives, or people in service of some kind or other.

It was huge. There were one or two people still living there, and a family or two; but the main apartments were closed after grandmother had left and mother and father had found the fifteen room *Selāmlik* (literally: the place for exchanging greetings – understood to be males) large enough for their abode, and only kept rows and rows of trunks there, all locked and all covered in yards of dust cloths. There was very little furniture in it and whenever the trunks were opened for airing or taking something out, we, the children, were quickly sent out so as not to breath the dust. I remember the view, surreptitiously seen from low-silled, tall windows, of a magnificently exposed Bosphorus in brilliant sunlit blue, serenely flowing its tortuous way down towards the Seraglio point, while to the north the view took in the upper Bosphorus wending a narrower way between the two castles of Europe and Asia.

For me the trunks were like treasure trove; ancient embroideries of birds and flowers, shawls, materials, laces, fabrics. I inherited some of these. I remember very specially the many coloured stiff silk lengths, two ends of which were tied round the waist of some person while the other two corners were gathered in the left hand, thus forming a large pouch in which were thrown a heap of many-coloured shiny cornets, about eight to nine inches long. These were prepared by the famous Haci Bekir, the sweet shop *par excellence* of Istanbul, famous for its many wares. These cornets, however, held small boiled sweets of rose, lemon, mint, etc., and were distributed to all present on the occasion of the Prophet's Birthday. The man who carried them would dip into the silken cloth with his free hand and bring out a pair of these shiny paper cornets and deposit them gently by the side of each person. The *Mevlūd* (Prophet's Birthday) ceremony had a special allure and preparation for which the trunks of the upper house were opened. At these times, the furniture of our drawing room was removed and was replaced by huge mattresses encased in striped and embossed silk covers in brilliant but sober colours of gold upon purple, emerald, ruby, and dark blue narrow strips covering the soft mattresses lengthwise. For the readers of the *Mevlūd*, there was a 15th century text, written by Süleyman Çelebi of Bursa in verse, which had to be intoned by the readers, who were three; there was a double depth of mattress which raised them above the audience. These three readers were engaged for the quality of their voices, intonation and the stress with which they punctuated the poems. It was at the moment when the poem mentions that angels brought sweet-meats to the mother of the Prophet during the labour period of birth, that the cornets of sweets were deposited beside the listeners. At the mention of the cooling sherbet presented to the mother in labour by the angels, sherbets were brought in huge trays laden with Baccarat crystal sherbet cups with the knob on the cover in gold, as well as the handle, the lip of the cup, and its saucer. The coloured sherbet – usually pomegranate juice – and the sweets were my delight. So also was the whole preparation of the ceremony, although the lengthy listening to the chanted 15th century poem, which I did not understand in any way, was a bit tedious and fidget-inducing; especially tedious as one could not let oneself go into the limbo of sleep and sweets as one had to sit 'properly' and awake under the gaze of the seemingly endless number of elder eyes.

The preparations for this important Muḥammedan night would start a day or two before the date. There was a huge bronze chandelier in our big drawing room with candle-holder branches and tubular glass protectors from wind, each of which opened out at the end like a tulip. Each of the glass affairs had to be brought down, dusted, polished and reinstated with a new long candle in the holder. That night no electricity was turned on in the big room. A merrily flickering mellow light lit up the room in unexpectedly brilliant radiance which was both soothing and smooth. It was like a new sense of light for me. Light was not just light any more. Light varied, always helpful to see, but each of different quality to humour or haunt one, or lead one into a comfortable mood of delight, or simply drive one on to further toil and travail, relentless white, demanding light, altogether other than the deep 'bright affluence of bright essence increate', as Milton would put it.

The Story of a Town

The Sufi Emperor

AFTER the wonders of Agra, the fabulous capital of the Great
Moghuls, with its gems of architectural vestiges like the Taj
Mahal and the Red Fort, the road that stretches south-west-
wards across the Indian plain is unenticing. For some thirty
kilometres there is nothing to catch the eye, and scenes of peas-
ant life offer little variation. The varied hues of lush green
stretching as far as the eye can see offer no other alternative
but a dreamy, drowsy nonchalance.

Suddenly, a jagged cone of pink comes into view. Obviously
the hill is truncated and the top of the cone is replaced with
an orgy of reddish pink sand-stone buildings. A whole town,
complete with palaces and mosques, tombs and towers, girded
with walls and monumental gateways, stands abandoned,
empty except perhaps for a visitor in quest of solace, a tourist
come to see the glories of the past, or a dervish come to visit the
marble filigree tomb of the saint Salīm Chishtī. This is forsaken
Fatehpur Sikri, which lies like a dusty ruby in a sea of emerald.

No-one really knows why it was abandoned. There are, of
course, intelligible reasons proffered, like lack of enough water
to supply the demands of the one-time capital of the greatest
of the Great Moghuls of the Timurid line, which now 'lies',
as Fitch described it in the late 16th century, 'ruinate'. Others
say, less plausibly, that Agra was more central, so the emperors
returned to their original capital. Some again, discard it as of
no import, thinking of Fatehpur as Akbar's folly, where he
stayed a dozen years or so to hunt deer from a tower, and then
returned to Agra. But the truth may be quite different.

Sixteenth century India was finally settling down to a central-ised empire under the descendants of Tamerlane. Bābur had come into India to replace the rule of the Afghani chieftains who held the North of the sub-continent in their power. Bābur's son, Humayun, had succeeded his father, but had been ousted and had taken refuge in Persia. When he regained power, he had little time to unify his empire. The task was left to his son, Abdul Fattaḥ Jalaludin Muḥammed Akbar.

Akbar (1542–1605) inherited a hodge-podge of people for an empire when he came to the throne at the age of thirteen years and four months. There were the Muḥammedans, the Buddhists, the Hindus, the Jain, the Zoroastrians, and the later alteration of Nanak's disciples who were the Sikhs. Of course, there was a smattering of Jews and the contact with Christianity was already established. All this *pêle-mêle* of disparate people used separate languages, plus vulgate forms. On top of all this was implanted Persian as court language, with some Arabic because of the connotations with the religion of Muḥammed, and some Turkish, since the Moghul Emperors were of Turk-ish descent, like their predecessors, the Tuquq or like Mahmud of Ghaznī. When the Lodi dynasty from Afghanistan and the Afghan chieftains had taken over, they had brought in the Urdu language, which in itself is a mixture of Turkish and Persian. Under these circumstances, unification of India by force was always feasible; but then its maintenance would demand a con-stant and exhausting vigilance.

The ethnic and religious communities were, as always, in-clined towards separatist tendencies, prompted by the dogmatic and formalised religious exclusivity. Even the originally non-dogmatic religion preached by Muḥammed had acquired a for-malised exclusiveness of worship which belied its universality. However, the Muḥammedan mystics who had come into India with the advent of the Turkish rulers had found the atmosphere propitious to their esoteric beliefs and teachings, and their revulsion of the Muḥammedan doctrinary teachers (the *'ulamā'*)

98

prompted them to avoid large conglomerations of people, like the cities where the *'ulamā'* ruled alongside the government. The esoteric behaviour patterns of these mystics, known as Sufis, seemed to approach them closer to the Hindi or Buddhist hermits, and facilitated their acceptance by the common people of India, which had already familiarised itself with the existence of recluses, living a devotional life apart. Consequently, the Sufis were revered not only by the Muḥammedans but also the Hindus, who regarded them as saintly *gurus* or ascetics.

There were three main Sufi orders which flourished in this sympathetic atmosphere: that of Suhrawardi whose adepts were for the greater part in the Sind: that of Firdawsi, which was popular in Bihar: and a major one, mainly near Delhi itself, that of the Chishtī, among whose disciples were many well-known people such as the historian Barāonī and the poet Khusrau. The shrine of the founder of the order, Mu'in al-din Chishtī at Ajmer, was already a well-established place of pilgrimage to which people of all classes flocked for a prayer or plea, including Akbar, who already showed a marked Sufi inclination. As if by accident, at the time Akbar was ruling India, there lived a very highly venerated Sufi saint of precisely the Chishtī order, Shaykh Salīm Chishtī, who had a highly reputed esoteric centre at Sikri near Agra.

It was a personal tragedy that prompted Akbar to seek a Sufi teacher, and consequently attempt to find a unifying solution for his disparate country in esotericism.

When his twin sons died at an early age, and he seemed to beget no other children, Akbar was disconsolate. As his devotion to the Chishtī was genuine, he pledged a pilgrimage on foot to Ajmer if he ever had children again. The saintliness of Salīm was well known to the court, and Akbar expressed the wish that he would also see Salīm. The Chishtī Shaykh was at the time living a life of retirement and retreat. There was no way of bringing him to Agra except against his will and by force. Akbar refused to oblige the venerable Salīm to be brought to him, and decided instead to pay a visit to the saint himself. Muḥammed would go to the mountain!

The meeting took place in great splendour and with great respect shown by Akbar to the white-haired holy man. As those who know the customs of the Sufis will understand, from then on Akbar recognised Salīm as his teacher in esoteric knowledge. This means a voluntary submission of self-will to that of one's 'enlightener' (*murshīd, guru*), or guide, and thus Akbar became a student (*murīd*) of Salīm Chishtī.

Such an occurrence is not unique in the annals of Oriental rulers. Mehmet II of the Ottomans, the Conqueror of Constantinople, also had a similar guide in Shaykh Ak Shamseddin in the 1450's. But it was the first time ever that esoteric learnings acquired by a sovereign were to be applied to the unification of a motley of people in a state. However, that was to come. The immediate result of the meeting was that soon after, as promised, Akbar's first and oldest wife was sent with a large retinue to live in the devotional centre (or *Ashram*, as they were called in India) where Salīm taught and presided in Sikri.

The child, a boy, was born to Miriam on the 30th August in Sikri. At once the customary proclamations were sounded, food and alms were distributed to neighbours and the poor, and celebrations continued for several days. The happy news was sent *post-haste* to Akbar, who was holding court in Agra. Delighted, Akbar named his son Salīm in honour of his teacher (the young Salīm later succeeded his father to the Timuride throne, and is known to history as Jahangir). Soon after, Akbar had other children, sons and daughters, the eldest of whom was another boy called Murad. The time had come to fulfil his votive pilgrimage on foot to Ajmer, and on the 20th January 1570 Akbar set out for the shrine of Muʿin al-din Chishtī. On the 23rd September, we find Akbar again at Ajmer, this time for his annual pilgrimage, having remained only twelve days at Sikri, where the first foundations of a new city were laid out. It was to be called Fatehpur, the city of Victory or Opening Up.

Akbar's own name was Abdul Fattaḥ, the Servant of the Victorious or the Opener, an attribute of God. The allusion in the name of the new city was two-fold.

Next year, on July 24th, Akbar was again in devotion at Muʿin al-din Chishtī's shrine at Ajmer, and on August 9th back at Fatehpur to speed up the building of the new capital. Abul Fazl, his constant companion and secretary, who with his brother Faizī recorded everything Akbar did in the famous *Akbar-namah*, says the following: 'In as much as his (Akbar's) exalted sons had been born at Sikri and the God-knowing spirit of Shaykh Salīm had taken possession thereof (of Sikri), his (Akbar's) holy heart desired to give outward splendour to this spot which already possessed spiritual grandeur. Now that his standards had arrived at this place, his former design was pressed forward, and an order was issued that the superintendents of affairs should erect lofty buildings for the use of the Emperor'. Nor was Akbar satisfied with order given. He personally supervised the 'lofty' and other buildings to hasten the 'outward splendour' he wanted to bestow on Fatehpur Sikri.

Akbar was in those days still at the learning stages of awareness which would eventually bring him to realise fully the Absolute Being whose Divine Essence permeates all His infinite Manifestations. For this is what the Sufis believe, and the complete realisation of this by the lifting away of the successive veils until total recognition is achieved of Complete Truth, the Reality of Realities, or the Perfect Man, a tangible manifestation of which is Muḥammed, after whom Akbar himself was named. It is not an easy path, and the methods used are constant Recalling (known as *zikr*), Meditation (known as *ṣalāt*), Volition coupled with Acquisition of Knowledge, which involves trust in the teacher, and at the last, 'lowest' level, though nonetheless as important as the other three, Service, because all service is ultimately service to God. These four are considered as naturally necessary conditions, *sine qua non*, of a proper lover. Because the Sufi way is the way of Love, as Love is the primal motive in manifestation, it requires great strength of character and constancy. The life this system imposes is both of a contemplative as well as of a man 'in the world'. The two aspects of the Absolute Being, the Transcendent and the Immanent, would have to be perfectly balanced. Akbar neglected neither side. Akbar had accepted well the Jesuits, who, after their disappointment in failing to Christianise Akbar had become rather harsh in judgement against him; nevertheless, they attest that '… he lived in fear of God, to whom he never failed to pray four times daily.'

Equally, on the worldly plane, Akbar was indefatigable. Born on 14th October 1542, he was a mere stripling when he came to the throne in 1556, and had to put up with the tutelage of his old friend, Bairām Khān. But even at this early age, there were pointers to what Akbar's character would be. When he began consolidating the Empire, the Adili Dynasty, which claimed descent from the brother of the Ottoman conqueror of Constantinople, Mehmet II, was naturally wary that Akbar might extend his rule beyond the southern boundaries of Delhi. To forestall such an eventuality, Hemū, the champion of the Adili South, met the forces of Akbar's Bairām on the plains of Panipat, where thirty years beforehand the first Moghul, Bābur, Akbar's ancestor, had wrested the crown of India in the famous battle of Panipat. Now the Moghul forces under Bairām were again aligned against the much-superior forces of Hemū in the same place, and the issue was for the same stakes.

If it had not been for the accident which fixed an enemy arrow into the eye of Hemū, the subsequent history of India might have been quite different. Unlike Harold at Hastings in 1066, Hemū did not die of the wound. Instead, he quickly yanked the arrow out of his eye and continued to fight bravely as if nothing had happened. But it was of no avail. Soon he was overpowered. Savagely wounded and gory, he was brought by Bairām before the young Akbar. Bairām asked the Emperor to kill Hemū on the spot, instantly. Akbar admired valour, and would have preferred to forgive Hemū and annexe the friend-ship of the valiant foe to his own forces. Bairām, without wait-ing for permission from his sovereign, drew his sword and killed Hemū on the spot, saying that too much compassion would lose the Empire. Akbar never forgave the terrible deed. He bided his time, and in about four years he found the means of sending Bairām away with an honourable discharge, on a pilgrimage to Mecca to expiate his sins.

Akbar now had taken the reigns of government into his own hands. At this time, he had only the Punjab with the provinces of Delhi and Agra as his Empire. Four years before his death, at the age of sixty, Akbar ruled and reigned over all of India which lies between Kashmir and the Narmada, and between Assam and Afghanistan, down to the Salaiman Mountains. He had assembled an enormous territory, a great multitude of people of all backgrounds and extraction, an incalculable wealth, and a renown as the 'Great Moghul', which echoed his name (Akbar = the Greatest).

Akbar's greatest achievement, however, was the utopian Fatehpur, which was also his greatest failure. Here, Akbar had built a new capital, just as resplendent as Agra, both bigger than the London of the times. The market extended non-stop between the two distant towns, Agra and Fatehpur Sikri. Fatehpur was all in pink-red limestone, every inch of it beauti-fully worked, carved and decorated. Areas of terracing were incorporated into the constructional plan. All the best architects were used. Indian art, renewed and adapted, found a revived, superlative expression. Akbar gave possibilities of income to many, so that they too should build and embellish Fatehpur. Like Constantine the Great, who asked all the patricians of Rome to build a replica of their houses in the New Rome which was Constantinople, Fatehpur became a riot of constructional splendour. Here, again, like the Christian Emperor had wished to a do, a new spiritual concept was meant to flourish.

But it did not. Akbar was not of his time. A new religion is easier to establish where masses are concerned. A mystical way of thought requires spiritually and mentally enlightened media through which to establish an esoteric level in which to flower. The Sufi concept of the all-permeating Unity which is the Absolute Essence, was beyond the reaches of the general levels of his time. In fact, the idea underlying Fatehpur is barely coming into fruition today. In the days of Akbar, anything so informal, so intangible, was incomprehensible to the masses. A thought process, no matter how akin to Reality as that of the Sufis, all inclusive and supra-religious, was only looked upon as incompatible with the hereto exclusive and dogmatic formality of religions. On 26th June, 1579, when Akbar personally read the *khuṭba* (an address read to the Friday congregation before the prayer starts), it should have indicated to him the profound truth of what was said in the last two lines: 'His attributes transcend man's understanding. Exalted be His Majesty! God is the most Great! (*Allāhu Akbar!*)' The gathered masses only thought Akbar was talking about himself! Transcendence of God was beyond their understanding, the immanence of the sensible world was the sole concern of the *'ulamā'* and the congregation, the establishment.

1580 marked the first of many outbreaks against Akbar. The *'ulamā'* and the orthodox Muḥammedans saw in Muḥammed Ḥakīm, the worthless King of Kabul, Akbar's own brother and vassal, their champion. However, the riots were quelled, everyone was forgiven and in the 1582 the Sufi way of thought was more or less painfully formalised and was called a new religion: *Dīnī Ilāhi* (Divine Religion). Though the effort was and seemed impossible, some good was achieved. In 1583, the Department of Religious Affairs included the Office of 'Suppression of Bigotry' for all religions and their practices, including the Hindi, where the sacrifice of the wife at the husband's death was forbidden.

Akbar had come a long way in Fatehpur, where he built a large pavilion known as the *Dīwānī Khaṣṣ* (Private Audience).

104

He had people of all religions come, discuss and argue their beliefs and their differences. From 1568 to 1600, Jesuits from Portuguese Goa were constantly at court in the hope of Christianising Akbar and his realm. But what they, and nearly everyone else, did not understand, was that Akbar was not necessarily looking for a new religion. He was simply coaxing all leading religious thinkers of all religions to bring forth and expose the common underlying mystical and esoteric foundations upon which all religions are built, no matter how disparate in practice. In the middle of the *Diwānī Khaṣṣ* there was an elaborate column which rose to the height of the second floor and which opened up at that level into a circular platform like a flower, for Akbar to sit and listen to the arguments below. Stonework screens shielded the four bridges of access from the four corners of the hall as well as the circular platform, so that no-one could know if Akbar was actually listening or not. Through the teachings of Salīm Chishtī, Akbar had personally developed enormously in esoteric thought by 1579, and was already accepted and referred to as the *Jagad-guru* (World Teacher of Humanity). But humanity did not follow him. Established ways were difficult to give up, and the establishment and the *'ulamā'* saw to it that 'humanity' did not. Akbar had tried, surely aware towards the end that he would fail, and had failed. When the King of Balkh, Abdullah II, sent an envoy to enquire into the peculiar religious aims of Akbar, the Great Moghul answered with an impromptu quatrain:

'Of God people have said that He had a son,
Of the Prophet some said, "He is a sorcerer".
Neither God nor the Prophet have escaped man's slander;
Then, how should I?'

In 1584, Akbar left Fatehpur. Salīm Chishtī died, and his presence and *baraka* (spiritual and temporal bounty) was no more there. Curiously enough, it was on the 21st June that same year, on the day of Nawruz, that a 'Divine Era' had been proclaimed. It seemed that the great Shaykh Salīm Chishtī would be no party to it. A Sufi cannot be bound by a form. Akbar understood the value of the loss implied. He left Fatehpur forever, and returned with his court to Agra, his former capital, after having ordered a lovely marble filigree tomb for his teacher in the courtyard of the great Mosque at Fatehpur. His idea was that there be nothing but Peace to surround the tomb of Salīm. Peace be upon them both!

A Short Bibliography

Translations

Fusus al-Hikam
Ismail Hakki Bursevi's Translation of and Commentary on *Fuṣuṣ al-Hikam* by Muhyiddin Ibn 'Arabī. Rendered into English by Bülent Rauf with the help of R. Brass and H. Tollemache.
Muhyiddin Ibn 'Arabī Society, Oxford and Istanbul. Vol 1, 1986; Vol 2, 1987; Vol 3, 1989; Vol 4, 1991.

Kernel of the Kernel
Ismail Hakki Bursevi's Translation of *Lubb al-lubb* by Muhyiddin Ibn 'Arabī. Translated from Turkish by Bülent Rauf.
Beshara Publications, 1981. Reprinted 1997.

Mystical Astrology According to Ibn 'Arabī
By Titus Burckhardt. Translated from the French by Bülent Rauf.
Beshara Publications, 1977. Reprinted 1989.

Books

The Last Sultans
A history of the closing period of the Ottoman Empire.
Published privately by Meral Arim, Gloucestershire, 1995.

Addresses
Eleven addresses originally written for students of the Beshara School of Intensive Esoteric Education, together with the paper 'Union and Ibn 'Arabi'.
Beshara Publications, 1987.

Great Dishes of the World in Colour
Edited by Jennifer Feller. Hamlyn, London, 1976.
The section on the Eastern Mediterranean is by Bülent Rauf. Each section was originally planned as a separate volume.

Articles & Others

Turning
A film produced and directed by Diane Cilento, 1975.
Historical adviser, contributor to the script, and one of the narrators for the film.

Union *An Address to the Symposium on Humanity.* The Beshara Trust, 1979.

Concerning the Kernel of the Kernel *Beshara News Bulletin, Summer 1981.*

Response to Sheer Beauty *Beshara News Bulletin, Summer 1985.*

Union and Ibn 'Arabī *Journal of the Muhyiddin Ibn 'Arabī Society, Vol III, 1984.*

Universality and Ibn 'Arabī *Journal of the Muhyiddin Ibn 'Arabī Society, Vol IV, 1985.*

Wisdom and Wisdoms *Journal of the Muhyiddin Ibn 'Arabī Society, Vol V, 1986.*

Concerning the Universality of Ibn 'Arabī *Journal of the Muhyiddin Ibn 'Arabī Society, Vol VI, 1987.*

To Suggest a Vernacular . . . *Beshara Magazine, No 1, Spring 1987.*

A Consideration since Assisi *Beshara Magazine, No 1, Spring 1987.*